The Victoria County History
1899–2012
A Diamond Jubilee Celebration

The Victoria County History
1899–2012
A Diamond Jubilee Celebration

JOHN BECKETT, MATTHEW BRISTOW, ELIZABETH WILLIAMSON,

WITH CONTRIBUTIONS FROM COUNTY COLLEAGUES

Second edition
First published 2012

A Victoria County History publication

© The University of London, 2013

All images © University of London except where stated.

ISBN 978 1 905165 91 9

Cover image: *Part of a promotional leaflet issued during the First World War by the General Editor, William Page, to advertise some of the distinguished contributors to the wide range of subjects covered by the VCH.*

Back cover image: *Map showing the counties already covered by the VCH. Red represents counties with work in progress, grey the counties where no work is underway in 2012; only Northumberland has no VCH volumes.*

Typeset in Minion Pro by Jessica Davies

CONTENTS

THIS HISTORY IS DEDICATED BY GRACIOUS PRIVILEGE TO

QUEEN ELIZABETH II

IN CELEBRATION OF HER MAJESTY'S DIAMOND JUBILEE,

AND INSCRIBED TO THE MEMORY OF HER LATE MAJESTY

QUEEN VICTORIA

WHO GRACIOUSLY GAVE THE HISTORY ITS TITLE

The dedication to Her Majesty the Queen to be printed in all VCH red volumes from 2012.

FOREWORD

As a history undergraduate in Cambridge, I would get up early each Saturday morning to make sure that I was at David's Bookstall in Market Square as they put out the second-hand books. It was there that I first came across the work of Laurence Gomme, statistical officer and subsequently Clerk at the new London County Council, and found myself buying his books on London. Gomme was the founding inspiration for the Victoria County History, as well as persuading the LCC to adopt the Blue Plaque scheme. It is fitting that page 10 of this fascinating volume shows the plaque erected in his honour on the house that was his home during the years in which he not only helped shape the London County Council and continued his work as a prominent folklorist, but also dreamed up the Victoria County History.

My undergraduate years passed and I started a doctoral thesis on London history. It was then that I discovered Gomme's greatest legacy, the Victoria County History. As I looked at volumes from different periods of the VCH's evolution, I found myself fascinated on the one hand by the richness of the information and insights that filled its pages, and on the other by the way the VCH remade itself time and again since it was founded in 1899. I could not but be impressed by the way each volume reflected the historical fashions of its time while holding to its ambition to build a history of England through the history of its counties.

I would never have expected, as I scoured David's Bookstall for bargains and picked up volumes by Gomme, that years later I would be the Vice-Chancellor of London's great University in the year of the VCH's rededication by Her Majesty the Queen. The ability of the VCH continually to reinvent itself, to adapt to changing historical questions and changing technologies, while remaining true to Gomme's founding vision, is one reason amongst many for the University of London to value its long association with the VCH. Since 1921 that association has been through the Institute of Historical Research (IHR), itself an indispensable support for historical research today.

For these reasons, and many more, I'm delighted to commend to readers this splendid publication. In this year of the Diamond Jubilee, the University is honoured that Her Majesty the Queen has graciously agreed to rededicate the Victoria County History. As the VCH looks forward to an exciting future, it is fitting that this volume gives us all the opportunity to consider its journey over the last 113 years. If historical scholarship does not reflect on its own past, then who will do so?

Geoffrey Crossick
Vice-Chancellor, University of London

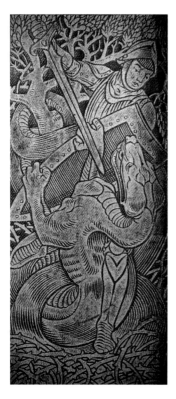

The spine of the first VCH volumes featured St George and the dragon.

The IHR is proud of its long association with the Victoria County History. When the Institute started life in 1921 — in prefabricated buildings in Bloomsbury — room was found for William Page, the History's General Editor. Then in 1933, the University of London formalised the arrangement, and ever since the two great institutions have been joined at the hip. Together with local authorities and universities up and down England, a series of enterprising publishers, and legions of loyal staff and volunteers the VCH has become one of the great academic publishing projects of the 20th century. The VCH stands alongside the History of Parliament and the Oxford Dictionary of National Biography as an indispensable resource for our national history. Through its red books, paperback volumes and now on its marvellous new website over one thousand years of local history come to life. All aspects are there: architecture, topography and landscape, religion, and the social and economic life of the parish.

Already the VCH has passed two significant anniversaries: in 1999 the centenary of its founding and in 2008 its 75th year at the Institute. Now in 2012 it passes another milestone. One of the many schemes and projects directly inspired by Queen Victoria's Diamond Jubilee in 1897, the VCH is now being rededicated by Her Majesty the Queen in her own Diamond Jubilee year. It is a good moment to reflect on the origins of the VCH, on the highlights and personalities of its long career, and the substantial achievements and findings of the county histories. This little volume, assembled with all the erudition, care and house-style for which the VCH is famed, does all that and more and makes a wonderful read.

It goes without saying that times were very different when the VCH came forth following the last Diamond Jubilee. There was a new civic self-confidence around then following county and parish reorganisation in 1888 and 1894. Commercial publishing was in its heyday, with profits generated from bestselling serials and fiction being turned to supporting scholarly tomes. And public awareness of national history was growing. This was especially noticeable at the regional level with the boom in the archaeological study of Roman Britain, and the efflorescence of local history societies matching the professional example set by the Royal Historical Society (1868) and the empirical and scientific turn in historical research at the principal universities. Out of this milieu came the VCH, co-founded by a publishing entrepreneur, Herbert Arthur Doubleday, whose firm Constable & Co. included Sir Arthur Conan Doyle on its books, and Laurence Gomme, statistical officer at the new London County Council. It is salutary to recall that the VCH was an entirely commercial and voluntary project for so many years before a public funding subsidy became available.

Now, as the VCH enjoys a special renaissance in the year of the Diamond Jubilee, once more we find the project having to make its way with all the guile and perseverance demonstrated by its founders. In the last decade the series has undoubtedly gone from strength to strength, not least due to the infusion of support from the Heritage Lottery Fund (HLF). But the vital input of the universities and the local authorities has waxed and waned, as other priorities for public spending in a new age of austerity have mounted. The VCH is increasingly returning to its roots. With volunteer researchers, indefatigable local fundraising committees and grants from charitable foundations, the VCH is alive and well in hard times. Such resilience is a testament to our fascination with the past in this old country, and a great credit to the many thousands of women and men who have made the VCH queen of local history.

Miles Taylor
Director, Institute of Historical Research

An English Heritage blue plaque dedicated to Gomme. It can be found at 24 Dorset Square, Marylebone NW1.

EARLY YEARS OF THE VCH

The VCH was founded in spring 1899 when Laurence Gomme, a well-known ethnographer, approached Arthur Doubleday, a partner in the publishing company Archibald Constable & Co., 'with a proposal for a County History'. Quite what Gomme originally proposed we do not know, but Doubleday subsequently recalled that he and Gomme had 'many discussions' during which Gomme's 'original idea was very greatly elaborated'. By the time the VCH was launched it had become a scheme for 'the compilation of a history of each county of England on a plan distinct from that adopted by the older historians'. In time it was believed that this would become a collective account of the localities amounting to 'a National Survey…tracing…the story of England's growth…into a nation which is now the greatest on the globe'.

Although this looks to the 21st-century eye to be an astonishing undertaking, it fitted with a late-Victorian trend towards major publishing projects. The VCH may have been a remarkable undertaking in its scope and breadth but it was by no means alone as a grand project. *The Dictionary of National Biography* had provided a blueprint for a successful collaborative, multi-volume venture, and it was followed by the *Oxford English Dictionary*, and the Survey of London, all functioning on similar principles. Gomme may even have had something similar to the Survey in mind, given that this was another project with which he was involved. To gain credibility for the project, Doubleday persuaded the Marquess of Lorne to seek out the approval of Queen Victoria to whom he wished the series to be dedicated. The original dedication appears in the very first volume *Hampshire* I. Subsequent volumes, which appeared after the Queen's death were inscribed to her memory, 'in the hope that it may prove a worthy memorial of her illustrustrious reign'.

The VCH was set up as a private enterprise, and it did not come into the public domain until its ownership was transferred to the University of London in 1933. It depended, a little like contemporary journals and magazines, on the publisher taking the risk by contracting (and paying) contributors, and recouping the company's outlay — and making a profit — through sales. Clearly it was on a different scale, given the intention of publishing 160 volumes covering every county, but Doubleday persuaded Constable's that it was a viable proposition, and he became the first General Editor.

Constable's could not fund the project from their own capital, but through his links in the publishing world Doubleday obtained a subsidy of £20,000 from Sir Osmond E. D'Avigdor-Goldsmid. This was a start, and a limited company was formed to run the VCH. Doubleday hoped to appeal to the local patriotism of those seen as potential sponsors and patrons who, as long as they bought the whole county set, would have their names included in the last volume for the county to preserve for all time the record of their patronage. In this way funds would be raised in advance to pay the authors, and the outlay would be recouped through sales. Somewhat optimistically, or so it now seems,

Doubleday at one point anticipated the project being completed in six years, with a profit of £250,000. In retrospect this was way off the mark, but it hints at the thinking in 1899.

Doubleday's business plan for the VCH may have been accepted by Constable's, but it bore little relationship to any reality. With virtually no dedicated infrastructure in Constable's London office, Doubleday was expected to start the project in all 40 English counties (including Monmouth) simultaneously, and to drive it so as to produce at least 16 (itself a figure scaled down from the optimism of 1899) volumes annually. In 1938, when he was able to look back on the early days with some dispassion, Doubleday admitted that such a vast project 'was a fight for time', in which getting the volumes into print and generating 'a sufficient literature output of high quality' had to be achieved quickly, and certainly 'before finance began to be exhausted.'

The most obvious problem was that, although authors were paid on acceptance of their work, the volumes did not appear quickly enough to recoup the outlay. In 1900 the VCH was turned into the 'County History Syndicate, Limited', a private limited company. William Maxse Meredith became the managing director and the only additional director was D'Avigdor-Goldsmid. The nominal share capital was £15,000. The directors were authorised to raise loans, particularly by the issue of debentures. By 1906 they had created debentures to the nominal value of £75,000, of which £51,800 had actually been issued. Also in 1906 D'Avigdor-Goldsmid advanced £50,000 as a loan to the company.

The VCH simply could not produce the volumes quickly enough to develop a steady income from which to pay the bills. William Page was brought in as joint General Editor in 1902, and when Doubleday left the VCH and Constable's in 1904, he became sole editor. He reorganised the office and the structure of research, writing and production, succeeding in the process in raising the number of volumes published annually. He could not achieve the magic figure of 16 volumes a year, largely because he did not have enough text to publish. At the same time costs were increasing, mainly due to a change in the method of funding the topographical work. Long lists of subscribers had been compiled, but they were required only to pay for the volumes they purchased, not for the county set as a whole. As Doubleday later reflected, 'remunerative subscriptions would not come in until volumes began to appear'.

The idea behind the VCH was simplicity itself, but the process of setting up the various county committees, appointing editors and contracting authors, quite apart from working out the content of both the general and the topographical volumes, meant that it was in financial difficulties from the outset. The first great financial crisis descended in 1908, at which point the project was nearly abandoned altogether. It was revived in 1910, closed because of wartime conditions in 1915, revived in a much attenuated form in 1922, transferred to the University of London in 1933, and reordered after 1945. It is now a national institution, run on completely different lines to the manner in which it was set up, and differently funded, but the principles behind it are still those originally discussed by Doubleday and Gomme in 1899.

A selection of red books in a stack. The evolution of their design is clear when they are viewed together in this way.

ORGANISATION

Initially the London office was part of the premises of Archibald Constable & Sons, of which Doubleday, the first General Editor remained an active partner. If this was the hub of the organisation, it was not where the work took place.

Doubleday recognised two major issues. The first was for the VCH to gain widespread acceptance for what it was trying to do, and the second was to create an organisation in which a central office would co-operate harmoniously with local historians and others in the counties.

With support from the Marquess of Lorne, Queen Victoria's son-in-law, with whom he had struck up a friendship, Doubleday was able to set up an Advisory Council, renamed in 1901 the General Advisory Council. It included three dukes, two marquesses, two earls, a viscount, two barons, two bishops, the President of the Royal Society, the Director of the British Museum, the Keeper of the Public Records, the Director of the National Portrait Gallery, the Director General of the Ordnance Survey, and the Regius chairs of History at Oxford and Cambridge. The purpose of the Council was to bring lustre to the project. Although it held a meeting in 1903, the Council was not primarily a working body; rather, it was an honorific group designed to convince the wider world of the importance of the project.

The real work of the VCH in London was entrusted to two committees, for Records and for Architecture. The Records Committee included well-known scholars such as Sir Frederick Maitland, H. Maxwell Lyte, J. Horace Round and W.H. Stevenson. Doubleday also appointed section editors for the different subjects covered in VCH volumes.

Doubleday recognised that the VCH could not be written exclusively in London, and that it would be necessary to 'combine harmoniously with local workers', both for the expertise they could provide and, as a publisher, for being the local experts whose names would help sell the books to the local gentry. He recognised as well that he needed to distinguish the VCH from the antiquarian tradition that at least some of these men represented. He needed, in his own words, an organisation which would 'have the twofold effect of obtaining subscriptions and of inspiring with confidence the county archaeologists and others whose local knowledge would be needed to supplement the work of various experts at headquarters'.

He began this task by approaching one of the leading antiquaries in each county to be local editor or, in the initial phase, local organiser, responsible with Doubleday for recruiting a county committee and identifying local 'specialist' writers for the general articles. If possible they would contribute to their county on their own interest areas. As with the Advisory Council, the role of county committees was largely ceremonial. Doubleday particularly wanted landed gentry on the committee, to help 'gain access to private collections of MSS'. There was no obvious intention that the county committees should promote or initiate work, and potential members were assured that they would not be called on to fund the project. Nor indeed was there any obvious need for the committees even to meet, although the Hampshire committee did in 1899, and the Lincolnshire committee in 1902.

The first County Editors included some distinguished scholars in their own right, most of whom were leading figures in their county antiquarian and archaeological societies. They included Richard Saul Ferguson in Cumberland, Revd W.O. Massingberd in Lincolnshire, W.H. Farrer in Lancashire, Canon Thomas Taylor in Cornwall, and Herbert Malden in Surrey. W.P.W. Phillimore claimed to have been approached to edit Nottinghamshire, but then ignored!

AIMS AND PLANS FOR COMPLETION

The VCH was planned by Doubleday and Gomme as a complete series of 160 volumes. Each county was to be tackled in a number of volumes ranging from eight for Yorkshire to two each for the smallest counties. Most counties were to have four volumes, although Norfolk was given six, Kent and Lancashire five, and Bedfordshire and Cambridgeshire three; Rutland and Westmorland were given two each. The number was soon adjusted to 184. Among the alterations was an addition to Hampshire (largely to accommodate the Isle of Wight), and three volumes for London which had originally been treated only on a parish by parish basis within Middlesex and Surrey.

After some experimentation, it was agreed that each county should have two volumes of general essays, and one, two, or more, of topographical entries. Rutland and Westmorland were to have one volume of general essays and one of topographical entries.

Doubleday was particularly keen on the general volumes because he did not want the VCH to resemble earlier county histories which had been written place by place. He insisted on 'making a special feature of general articles which should bring into prominence the main characteristics of every phase of county life'. These characteristics were to include 'the study of the social, economic and industrial development of each county', and 'the history and expert description of all the important buildings, ecclesiastic, military and domestic, throughout the country'.

Possibly because of this thinking, much less attention was paid initially to the research and writing of what were called the 'Topographical Accounts of Parishes and Manors'. The research required for those, together with the method of compilation, had to be worked out as it went along.

The first volume to be published was *VCH Hampshire* I, which came out in 1900. It was followed by three volumes in 1901, three in 1902, and two each in 1903 and 1904. Output increased to six in 1905, nine in 1906 and nine in 1907, and a record (never surpassed) of 12 in 1908. Unfortunately the economics of the VCH had been based on producing 16 volumes a year. In 1901 Constable's were expecting the whole 160-volume set to be ready in eight years, with 40 supplementary and larger volumes, dealing with pedigrees, 'either within the same period or very soon afterwards'.

None of this bore any relationship to reality because the plan had never taken into account the productivity of the potential authors. When William Page became sole General Editor in 1904 he introduced new methods of working, and by an extraordinary feat of organisation and editing produced 33 volumes between 1906 and 1908. By 1908 28 counties had a first volume published and 20 counties had volume II published; 16 counties had both I and II in print. Only Cheshire, Northumberland, Westmorland, Wiltshire, and the West Riding of Yorkshire had not been started. The topographical volumes had proved harder to organise, and by the end of 1908 only Hampshire and Lancashire had a complete volume of topography in print.

What might look impressive to us was not enough for the publishers. During the course of 1908 it became clear that the project was running into choppy financial waters, and in December Page wrote to local editors to say that the publishing programme had temporarily stopped. According to Sir Charles Peers, the first Architectural Editor, writing many years later but recalling events in 1908, despite Page's 'brilliant' efforts 'then came a disaster for which he himself was in no degree responsible'. The funds had, in effect, run out.

The VCH remained dormant through 1909, but was revived early in 1910 as the result of a financial deal which permitted the restart of work in ten counties. Some further progress was made before the outbreak of the First World War, but in a number of counties active in 1908 work stopped, never to be resumed. Sadly vast quantities of work completed before the financial crisis were never published. Fortuitously the formation of the Royal Commission on Historical Monuments in 1908 offered opportunities to some of the architectural staff of the VCH, who moved to the new enterprise.

Financial support organised through the publisher W.H. Smith saw a revival in April 1910, when a new start was made. W.F.D. Smith had agreed to guarantee the interest on the loans made by the debenture holders, and W.H. Smith & Sons were to take over the printing of volumes and the debts of the Syndicate. By 1912 the President of the Society of Antiquaries was able to announce that, due to Smith's liberality, the VCH was back

These volumes make a personal appeal to every Englishman

THE VICTORIA HISTORY OF THE COUNTIES OF ENGLAND

SEVEN POINTS OF INTEREST

1.

THE VICTORIA HISTORY OF THE COUNTIES OF ENGLAND is one of the *greatest works ever attempted*, in extent, interest and importance, and the largest enterprise of its kind ever undertaken by private effort.

2.

Owing to the thoroughness of the work, it is safe to say that it is a definite finality in English local History, and that *its value will not diminish* as new generations are born to live in the land of their fore-fathers.

3.

The Editorial Staff and Contributors number many hundreds of *England's finest scholars*.

4.

There is *no Englishman* to whom it does not in some one or other of its features make a direct appeal.

5.

It will be the standard for all time, and also the nearest thing possible to supplying each Englishman with *a history of his own individual ancestors* and of his native land.

6.

It is a treasure for every English home and generation, unprocurable in years to come.

7.

The name of every subscriber for a complete County received whilst the work is in progress will *be printed in the last volume of that County*, making a permanent record.

No family name, no parish is there which has not its special interest for some living person.

'Seven Points of Interest' from an early promotional prospectus in the VCH archives.

on its feet, but in fact funding had been secured for only ten counties. The favoured ten were never named in correspondence, but judging by publications, they must have included Bedfordshire, Hampshire, Hertfordshire, Lancashire, London, Middlesex, Nottinghamshire, Somerset and Yorkshire.

When the First World War broke out research continued, although in conditions which created immense difficulties for the VCH. A researcher in Lancashire examining church bells was 'carried off to a police station two miles distant as a spy', while an Oxford don taking notes of the Roman wall 'had to be protected from an angry mob who took him for a spy'. Two members of the staff of the Royal Commission on Historical Monuments were taken to a police station in Essex under similar circumstances.

GENERAL VOLUMES

The two general volumes for each county were designed to cover common themes. As a publisher, Doubleday made no great claims to being an expert in any particular area, and so he recruited authors who could both write the necessary sections on a county-by-county basis, and others who could fill in the gaps when they occurred. Fortunately for Doubleday he knew many of the experts he initially recruited through his publishing connections and particularly through a magazine which he edited for Constable's, The Ancestor.

The subjects to be covered were established by Doubleday and Gomme from their earliest conversations. They would follow, loosely, a chronology from the beginning of history to the present time. Volumes I would cover Natural History (including geology), Prehistoric, Roman, and Anglo-Saxon Remains, Ethnography, Domesday Book, Architecture, as well as Ecclesiastical, Political, Maritime, and Economic and Social History, Industries, Arts, and Manufactures, the Feudal Baronage, Sport, Persons Eminent in Art, Literature, Science, and a bibliography. The topographical entries (initially undefined) would slot in after Domesday Book. In practice, not all of these subjects were undertaken. Ethnography was never covered; probably because Gomme left the project at an early stage. Feudal Baronage was dropped, the proposed 'modern Domesday' — an account of all owners of more than five acres of land — was not carried out, and Eminent Persons were covered not as separate articles but in the parish histories. Few general articles on architecture were published. New sections were occasionally added, including schools.

The subjects reflected Doubleday's concern, as a publisher, with the market for sales. He was relying on attracting the county families as purchasers of the volumes. The VCH had to attract the gentry as well as the leisured upper-middle and middle classes of society, and to cater for their interests in genealogy, heraldry and antiquities. Even the coverage of sport bore more relation to the interests of the presumed readership (hunting, fishing and shooting) than to the wider world, and so specialist subjects such as mountain climbing in Cumberland were rejected because they upset the uniform plan.

Some of the 'experts' appointed by Doubleday as section editors wrote a great deal while others were content to commission other writers. Several were scholars well known in their own disciplines, including the Romanist Professor Francis Haverfield.

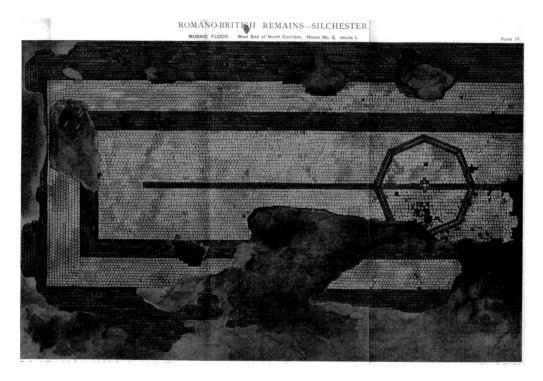

ROMANO-BRITISH REMAINS—SILCHESTER.
MOSAIC FLOOR.   West End of North Corridor, House No. 2, Insula I.   PLATE IV.

A Romano-British mosaic found at Silchester as illustrated in one of the remarkable fold-out illustrations in
VCH Hampshire I *(1900).*

Domesday Book was entrusted to the distinguished medievalist, J.H. Round. Originally
Round agreed to write the sections on Domesday Book for every county, but when he
was taken ill and could not continue, the work was undertaken by a young scholar, Frank
Stenton, who used the VCH as a stepping stone to develop his own academic career.
Round and Haverfield were prodigious writers, but for other sections experts needed to
be recruited by the VCH office, or locally. A number of scholars originally taken on as
County Editors contributed on their own specialist subjects, among them Ferguson on
earthworks and Wilson on ecclesiastical history in Cumberland, Massingberd on social
and economic history in Lincolnshire, Taylor on Domesday Book in Cornwall, H.E.
Malden on ecclesiastical and military history in Surrey, and J.W. Willis-Bund on various
aspects of natural history, ecclesiastical, political, industrial and agricultural history in
Worcestershire.

In the period until Doubleday resigned from the joint general editorship in 1904
only a single female contributor was acknowledged by name. This was Elizabeth Anne
Hodge, acknowledged as Sister Elspeth, who had studied in the Oxford honours school
of modern history. In spring 1903 she was working at the All Saints' Boys Orphanage
in Lewisham, London. She received permission from her Anglican Order, Sisters of
the Poor, to work on the religious history of one county as an experiment. She initially
preferred Norfolk, but had to settle for Bedfordshire. By spring 1904 she was working in
Lincoln on material relating to religious houses of the county. Then she was taken ill and
ordered to rest. In order to recuperate she sailed to America to stay in one of her order's

homes in Baltimore, and by November she was telling the VCH she was fit and well and happy to continue with her work on Lincolnshire and Buckinghamshire. She sent in her entry on Lincolnshire in June 1907 by which time she was working on Huntingdonshire, which she submitted in February 1909, and Rutland. She also wrote on Leicestershire. Of course, this way of working remotely was not ideal. It took a small army of workers in London to find and copy out the documents from which she needed the evidence to write up her work. Altogether Sister Elspeth wrote on six counties, contributing ecclesiastical history essays for five and religious houses essays for four. Her work on Huntingdonshire appeared only in 1926.

After 1904, when Doubleday left the VCH, attention was given to completing general volumes while topographical research was underway. To that end the VCH began to employ younger scholars at a fixed rate of one guinea per thousand words. Many of those recruited were women who found an appropriate opportunity to use their skills (see page 27 for more).

Natural history

The first section in the first general volume of each county set was natural history. Since the general essays were to cover the history of each county from the beginning until the present, this made sense especially as many of the county societies were responsible for natural, architectural and antiquarian history as well as archaeology. The VCH Advisory Council included the presidents of the Royal Society, the Linnean Society, and the Zoological Society, as well as the Director of the British Museum.

The first editor for natural history was Aubyn B.R. Trevor-Battye, a distinguished natural historian. He was offered £10 per county as editor of the natural history section, and £1 per thousand words for any text he contributed from his own pen. His commission was to deliver about 100 pages of approximately 500 words each, for each county. Trevor-Battye worked hard on the natural history, judging from the number of in-letters to him in the VCH archive, but for reasons now unknown he seems to have dropped out around 1902.

Trevor-Battye was not expected to do all the work himself. He was invited to write on subjects that interested him, and to recruit other specialists for areas outside his speciality. Richard Lydekker, a geologist and palaeontologist of long-standing reputation on the staff of the Natural History Museum, was a prolific natural history author, whose works included *A Manual of Palaeontology* (1889). He was recruited to write on palaeontology, and he prepared the entry for every county. His attitude was that this was a commercial undertaking, and when Trevor-Battye approached him in April 1900 he made it clear how he would operate:

> I presume the palaeontology includes only fossil mammals, birds, reptiles and fish, and excludes Invertebrates (which would be endless). If this is so, I think I can undertake what you require. In a county like Hants., which has a large fauna of fossil reptiles, I should require 4 pages to make it readable. But even if the publishers reduce this number to 3 pp. I should ask £2 2s for the contribution. Also a similar amount for other

counties with a large fauna. In the case of counties like Hertfordshire, where vertebrate fossils are scarce, a couple of pp. would probably suffice. A more usual scale of pay is £2 2s 0d per 1000 words, but in the above conditions (that is a minimum fee of £2 2s for the counties with large fauna) and the further proviso that payment is to be made within a month of having the proofs for press, I am willing to undertake the task.

The Reverend T.R.R. Stebbing of Ephraim Lodge, Tunbridge Wells, son of Henry Stebbing who had edited *The Athenaeum*, described himself as 'a serf to natural history, principally employed about Crustacea' and 'an early and enthusiastic convert to Darwinism'. He wrote the entries on crustaceans for all 40 counties.

Others contributed to a number of counties, including B.B. Woodward on non-marine molluscs for 28, and F.O. Pickard-Cambridge who wrote on spiders for 22. Some came and went more sporadically, including William Warde Fowler who contributed articles on beetles to ten counties. Reverand Edwin Bloomfield wrote regularly on insects. Detailed guidelines were worked out as to what should be included in each section of the natural history, and the nomenclature which was to be employed.

Table showing Victoria County History volumes which include natural history entries.

PUBLICATION YEAR	NUMBER OF VOLUMES	COUNTIES
1900	1	Hampshire
1901	3	Cumberland, Norfolk, Worcestershire
1902	3	Hertfordshire, Northamptonshire, Surrey
1903	1	Essex
1904	2	Bedfordshire, Warwickshire
1905	4	Buckinghamshire, Derbyshire, Durham, Sussex
1906	6	Berkshire, Devon, Cornwall, Lancashire, Nottinghamshire, Somerset
1907	1	Yorkshire
1908	5	Herefordshire, Kent, Rutland, Shropshire, Staffordshire
1911	1	Suffolk
1926	1	Huntingdonshire
1938	1	Cambridgeshire
1939	1	Oxfordshire
1957	1	Wiltshire
1969	1	Middlesex
1987	1	Cheshire
	Total 33	

The VCH recognised that in some cases there would be a local expert who could not be ignored. Unfortunately these contributors seldom had the attitude of a Lydekker, and their work was often slow to reach the London office and sometimes inadequate. The VCH wanted authors to summarise the state of knowledge, and to do so to a tight deadline, but trouble brewed with experts like Professor James Clark, Principal of the Truro Central Technical Schools, who single-handedly held up the production of *VCH Cornwall* I by insisting on undertaking new research into various species, notably of spiders, and then refusing to accept Page's editorial changes.

Once Trevor-Battye stepped down in 1902 he was not replaced by a single editor for natural history. Instead the subject was split up among a number of experts including Clement Reid and Horace R. Woodward for geology, Lydekker for palaeontology and, for the different branches of flora and fauna, G.A. Boulenger, F.O. Pickard-Cambridge, H.N. Dixon, G.C. Druce, Walter Garstang, Herbert Goss, R.I. Pocock, Stebbing, and others.

In total 27 counties had their natural history written before the First World War, amounting to something in the region of 1.4 million words. For many professional scientists it is a compendium of historical ecological knowledge which gives an understanding of environmental issues and different styles of plant and animal classification at the time. Subsequently the expansion of natural history knowledge became so overwhelming, and the emergence of specialisms in academic biology so rapid, that the VCH was no longer relevant to the needs of the naturalist, hence the effective abandonment of this section when new work began in a number of counties after 1933. That should not detract from its importance to the world of natural history between its foundation in 1899 and the outbreak of the First World War, or its interest for 21st-century naturalists who wish to discover the species prevalent in a particular county during those years.

ARCHAEOLOGY AND ARCHITECTURE

Serious study of the historic environment now includes as essential components archaeological monuments and buildings. But when the VCH was founded and as it evolved in the early years of the 20th century — when VCH workers bicycled around England inspecting churches and earthworks, and when the General Editor (ever ready to adopt the latest technology) hoped to equip them with motor-bicycles — it was far less obvious how archaeology and buildings should be incorporated into existing agendas of historical research and presented to the public in handsome books.

The early VCH put the study of archaeology and architecture alike on newly professional footings. It avoided rehashing second-hand interpretations, insisting on active fieldwork by well-trained investigators. Probably most significant was the VCH's influence on the Royal Commissions on Ancient and Historic Monuments for England, Scotland, and Wales, set up in 1908 to record monuments which pre-dated 1700 and to make recommendations for their preservation. Correspondence shows just how much the VCH provided a model for the Commissions: they shared key personnel (both advisory and professional) and an arrangement by county and parish. Perhaps most important, the VCH showed that it was possible to embark on an ambitious programme of scholarly investigation across the whole of England.

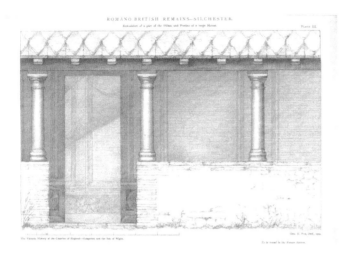

Reconstruction of the portico of a large Roman house at Silchester from VCH Hampshire I *(1900). It was drawn by George E. Fox, whose innovative work there between 1890 and 1909 with William St John Hope is seen as perhaps the first, modern, interdisciplinary excavation project.*

Archaeology

The VCH aimed to offer an archaeological synthesis for each county, setting out what was known, period by period. The volumes published before 1914 were typically the best syntheses then available, and in many counties the only ones. Much of their success was down to planning and personnel. The framework was apparently the work of three men: Charles Peers (Architectural Editor of the VCH 1903–10, before his appointment as Inspector of Ancient Monuments); A.G. Chater (honorary secretary of the Congress of Archaeological Societies); and especially William Page, the VCH's General Editor. National experts in particular areas were drawn in as archaeology editors, such as F.J. Haverfield on Roman Remains and Hercules Read on Anglo-Saxon; other contributors included Cyril Fox and E.T. Leeds. Clergy, schoolteachers and members of archaeological societies were signed up as helpers, and professional 'investigators' were engaged in 1909. A large proportion of the intended chapters appeared before 1914, and as a result the VCH helped to shape and redirect the study of English archaeology.

Architecture

Architecture also played a large part in the early VCH, not least because the founders saw how attractive volumes full of high-quality illustrations of buildings would be to subscribers. The serious study of church architecture was well established by 1900, a pioneering book on the English house had appeared in 1898, and summer outings to churches and mansions under expert guidance were a staple of the county archaeological societies. The initial plan was to treat buildings in two complementary ways: county surveys and detailed parish-by-parish descriptions. In the end only four county-wide chapters were commissioned and only two (Surrey and Sussex) were published: the over-ambitious idea was abandoned after Charles Peers became Architectural Editor in 1903, partly for lack of well-qualified authors and partly because it was premature to summarise before the mass of individual descriptions had been completed.

Instead, the effort was switched to an even more ambitious plan to provide detailed historical and architectural accounts of churches, manor houses, castles and other

Redrawn sketch of Lamer House in Wheathampstead (Herts.), published to accompany the history of Lamer manor in VCH Hertfordshire II (1908). Wheathampstead was one of the three model parish histories written up, printed and circulated to the VCH's authors and editors in Doubleday and Page's Guide to the Victoria History of 1903. All three were heavily illustrated with line drawings and photographs. The provenance of the sketch is not given.

important houses in every one of the 9,615 parishes of the VCH. A team of staff architects (mostly young men with architectural training) was recruited, but Page and Peers also hired freelancers and allowed the grandees of the Architectural Advisory Committee to cherry-pick some buildings of national significance. Staff and freelancers alike were 'trained in the History, by the History, for the History'. The precisely observed architectural descriptions of buildings in the Edwardian VCH — systematic, consistent, tightly written, making use of documentary and pictorial evidence, and buttressed by measured plans and specially taken photographs — set new standards in architectural history and made buildings an integral element of parish history.

TOPOGRAPHY

The VCH is primarily known today for its topographical entries, but in the initial phase of its work the emphasis was on producing the general volumes and little thought was given to how the parish entries would be compiled. In the earliest plan of the VCH they were simply included as one topic among the many to be covered. Doubleday seems to have had a vague idea that parish histories could be written by local parish clergy.

This thinking can still be seen in the way, for example, that the Hampshire and Surrey 'sets' were constructed, with the topography sandwiched between natural history and archaeology at the start of each set, and with all other sections following. It was soon recognised that the topographical entries needed separate treatment but, just as importantly, the reorganisation of 1904 meant that the output of general volumes would need to be increased, and so for practical reasons it made sense to work on a division for each county into two general volumes and two or more topographical volumes.

Little initial thought seems to have been put into how the topographical entries would be written or even of what content they would have. Doubleday assembled a small group of experts to make recommendations. This included the genealogist and publisher W.P.W. Phillimore. For reasons unknown this initiative fizzled out; instead, John Charles

Cox was asked to prepare some models based on Northamptonshire parishes. Cox had written the standard guide to how to write a parish history, published originally in 1879, and still at that time in print.

Doubleday relied for advice on the VCH Record Committee, particularly William Page and W.J. Hardy, the partners in a London record agency. The initial plan was for Hardy to employ one of the record searchers registered to the agency to work through sources in the Public Record Office and British Library for the parishes in a particular hundred (in this case Alton, Hampshire). He was also to solicit help from a county expert — who would deal with the local records — and then add in the separately researched architectural detail to complete a parish entry.

This scheme was tried out in Hampshire and failed. Firstly the local expert, Reverend George Henniker-Gotley, vicar of Empshott, objected to being treated as a glorified research assistant and refused to hand over his work. After an acrimonious correspondence with Central Office, he was fired. Secondly, Constance Toulmin, the record agent hired to work in the PRO on the Alton sources, declared the task to be unmanageable in the way demanded of her and resigned.

After this ill-fated experience the VCH needed to think again. In those counties where it had appointed a local editor, it requested the person involved to mastermind the topographical work. In particular it anticipated the editor working with the local clergy to research and write the entries. It helped if he was a clergyman, and in Cumberland and Cornwall, among others, the County Editor undertook to write all the entries, with or without help.

Locally based clergy might research and write parish histories, but few of them had the resources to spend time in the PRO and British Museum. Searching these records was regarded as vital if the VCH was to be distinct from earlier county histories, and also to be seen as offering new information. In some cases the VCH was prepared to fund assistance for local editors. In April 1900 they offered to provide H.E. Malden, the Surrey local editor, 'with a colleague to do the record work'. Malden was requested to recommend an assistant, someone he felt 'inclined to work with', but he preferred to recruit his own help directly.

The real problem was the inefficiency involved in searching each PRO class for the parishes in a particular hundred. As the 1903 report prepared for the Advisory Council noted, 'the collection and classification of materials had to be commenced *de novo* and a special staff of record experts had to be organised on a scale much larger than could have been anticipated'. The report continued: 'it was found in the course of this research work that in order to exhaust the records for any one county it was necessary to calendar whole classes of records for all the counties simultaneously'. In other words, blanket searching of all the classes was needed so that the references to each parish could be collated, and it was necessary to start afresh for each hundred or parish, or even county.

To make this happen, William Page, as joint General Editor, was asked to recruit and train young men and women to search all the class lists and indexes in the PRO, and each time they found a reference to a particular parish to enter the reference on separate sheet of paper. The searchers also worked through the reports of the Historical Manuscripts Commission, read the whole of the *Dictionary of National Biography* for references to places, the manuscript indexes to the Notes of Fines and to the Recovery Rolls; examined large numbers of Inquisitions Post Mortem, guild and chantry certificates, uncalendared

The Court House, Long Crendon (VCH Bucks IV): an example of the many pen-and-ink drawings in early topography volumes. The Court House was restored by A.S. Gomme, son of Sir Laurence whose country home, The Mound, was in the village.

Chancery rolls, and Proceedings in the Prerogative Courts. They also extracted some of the PRO Lists and Index volumes.

At the end of each day the recruits returned to Orange Street where they collated the slips on a parish-by-parish basis. Once the classes had all been searched, together with the British Museum, Lambeth Palace Library and a number of other sources, references were available for every parish across the country.

The slips would then be sent to County Editors who could consult all the references available when they or their fellow researchers next visited the PRO, and so would not need to waste time searching the indexes. In a few cases local editors were ready and willing to do the topographical work themselves. All the slips were sent to Canon James Wilson, who had succeeded Ferguson in 1901 as the County Editor for Cumberland; Wilson wrote all the parish histories for the county, although none was ever published. Those slips were deposited in Carlisle Library, where they still reside. Canon Thomas Taylor signed up to do all the Cornwall topography. Unlike Wilson, who seems to have had the means to go to London occasionally, or to employ a record agent, Taylor could not hope to visit the PRO regularly from St Just, and VCH researchers copied out documents on his behalf.

In practical terms this method meant that the VCH had decided to search the topographical sources for all English counties before further work was attempted on the parish entries for any particular county. The knock-on effect was that the production of topographical volumes would have to wait until the searching had been completed for all parishes nationally. This would, inevitably, create a gap in the publishing schedule. To bridge the gap, the decision was taken to reorder the material in the the county sets. From this point onwards all the general essays appeared in volumes I and II of a county set (volume I only in Rutland and Westmorland), leaving topography to volumes III and IV.

The Orange Street staff who searched the indexes in 1903 to 1906 proved to be so adept that Page decided to train those who offered their services to draft parish histories. According to a report of 1903 he set about 'training a number of workers who are daily becoming better qualified to assist in preparing the material which experts will mould into shape'. By using record agents in this way, the intention was to ensure uniformity between counties, and methodical research from original sources, with full references given so that readers could check and follow up the origin of every statement.

Once it was clear that the staff could also draft the parish entries, the VCH moved towards asking County Editors simply to check them. Reverend William Oswald Massingberd, the Lincolnshire County Editor, was one of those involved in this process, and he frequently grumbled to his fellow antiquarian clerics in the county about the way in which the entries were put together and how documents were interpreted.

After the financial crash of 1908 the system was changed again. The London staff were made redundant, and County Editors like Massingberd, and Frank Stenton in Nottinghamshire, were offered use of the slips to write the parish histories, much as Wilson had done in Cumberland. Stenton undertook to write all the Nottinghamshire entries, but was subsequently diverted by other calls on his time and none were written. Massingberd completed quite a number, but they were never published.

WOMEN IN THE VCH

The decision to reorganise in 1903–4 had numerous ramifications, of which one of the most interesting was the decision to employ a great many young women. Some were on the staff at Orange Street, in which case they were working on making the slips from PRO and other sources, and then on drafting parish histories. Others were employed to write essays for the general volumes in each county set. In some cases they were both staff and, separately contractors. The decision to employ women was not positive discrimination. It was because women who had studied at Oxford and Cambridge (from which they could not graduate at that time), as well as London and St Andrews, found themselves with few employment opportunities other than teaching. A few young men were employed in similar roles and all the architectural staff were male, but it was the availability of women which proved crucial to how the VCH operated.

Page recruited staff, all of whom appear to have been women, initially to undertake the searching of catalogues in the PRO and elsewhere. Eleven women were employed in that work, and their numbers caused trouble at the PRO. In the autumn of 1904 S.R. Scargill-Bird, one of the PRO Keepers and a member of the VCH Records Committee, warned Page that 'the presence of so many ladies employed on the Victoria County Histories in the Legal Search Room is I am sorry to say causing great inconvenience to the general public and I therefore write to you, privately in the first instance, to ask

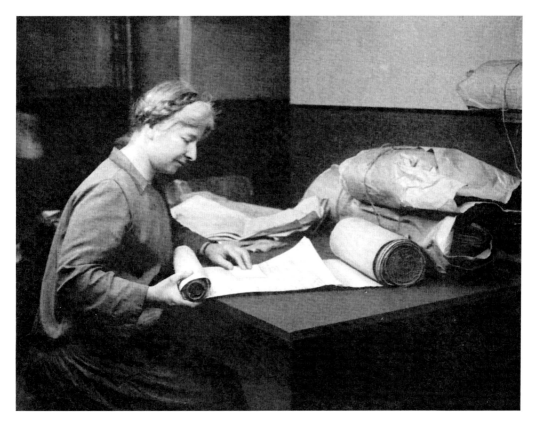

Lilian Redstone, seen here at the Public Record Office, worked for the VCH 1904–9, gained a London external degree in 1910, and subsequently became a record agent with a particular interest in her native Suffolk (image from Suffolk Farming in the Nineteenth Century *by Thirsk & Imray (1958), courtesy of Suffolk Record Society www.suffolkrecordssociety.com).*

whether you can reduce the number to more practicable limits'. Page was noncommittal in his reply and by May 1905 the VCH had 15 workers regularly in the PRO.

By this time the women were so well-trained that, rather than just passing on the slips to County Editors, as he had originally intended, Page gave them responsibility for drafting parish histories. He estimated as early as 1904 that he needed ten topographers, to 'proceed as fast as possible with the topography' of Cumberland, Hampshire, Hertfordshire, Northamptonshire, Surrey, Worcester and 'for boroughs', on the grounds that 'the record material ... is practically complete'.

At the same time, Page was keen to recruit young scholars on a contract basis to write general essays for the first two volumes in county sets, and again many of these were women. In 1904 he listed seven general articles he needed on ecclesiastical and political history for Derbyshire, Essex, Kent, Northamptonshire and Nottinghamshire. Women writers became the mainstay of contributions on ecclesiastical, economic and social, and political history, which were among the subjects covered in the second volume of each county set. Those who wrote on contract were offered the standard VCH rate of one guinea per thousand words, and were set tight deadlines for producing their material.

How many young women were employed in this work we do not know, but at least 100-plus have been identified working either as members of staff or as contractors, and at different times in both roles. Audrey Amy Locke (apparently she was Audrey in London but Amy in the country!) came from Winchester where she was a pupil at St Swithun's School. She then spent three years at Somerville before joining the VCH. She wrote general essays on politics for VCH Nottinghamshire I, religious houses for VCH Worcestershire II, and ecclesiastical history for VCH Cornwall II (unpublished), as well as topographical entries for VCH Hampshire III, IV and V, and VCH Worcestershire IV.

Not all the women employed on the VCH were willing volunteers. In October 1908 Miss Ada Hendy heard that work might be available but she was not exactly enthusiastic: 'Miss Wilmot tells me that you are prepared to offer me work on Hampshire. I should be willing to accept it on the understanding that I can at once give it up if I hear of something better.' Miss Hendy obviously did not manage to find a better job since she wrote Fareham, Titchfield, and co-authored Bermondspit for volume III (1908), and the whole of the New Forest Hundred for volume IV (1911) in the Hampshire series.

When the VCH financial crisis occurred in 1908 the women had to be dismissed, although when things were resolved in 1910 Page was able to rerecruit some of them. We know that a few were employed through 1914, 1915 and 1916, but we do not know who was on the staff and who was contracted during that period. Page was to claim later that by the time the First World War broke out he had recruited a staff of four sub-editors, four architects and over 40 research and clerical workers, all of whom had to be dispersed.

MOVE TO THE IHR

In 1918 the Syndicate established in 1900 to publish the VCH was declared bankrupt. No volumes appeared between 1915 and 1922 inclusive, and survival was in doubt. Page approached Oxford University Press in 1922 but, although that initiative failed, the second Lord Hambledon (of the W.H. Smith firm) agreed to buy the rights and cover general editorial expenses. According to Page: 'In 1922 to keep it alive the late Lord Hambleden who had previously been financially interested, generously purchased all the assets and rights and handed them to me to carry on in the best way I could'. Page had lived in Hampstead through the war years but when in 1922, in Charles Peers' words 'the whole burden of the History devolved on him, he removed to Middleton, near Bognor in Sussex, where he built a storehouse for the material, estimated to weigh fourteen tons.'

No funding was available for new work, but Page was able to encourage established scholars to write chapters for general volumes, and he himself edited for publication volumes which had been completed, or largely completed, before the First World War. Some projects had to be abandoned: the proposed volumes II and III of the London set never appeared, and new work on Middlesex remained in abeyance until the 1950s.

Then in 1931 came a further setback when the third Lord Hambleden withdrew support: as Page recalled, 'Lord Hambleden felt he could not continue the responsibility of the History and to save it from annihilation he permitted me to acquire it on favourable terms. I have no staff and have to find guarantors for the cost of the work I undertake on which, as in all work of the kind, there is necessarily a loss. I am however,

Senate House under construction. Building began in 1933, the year the VCH moved to the IHR which was then housed in a prefabricated building opposite the new site.

by means of these guarantees, able to keep the History alive.' Page managed to bring out 17 volumes between 1923 and 1932.

Hambleden sold the remaining rights to Page, who became owner as well as editor. Unfortunately Page's health was failing. He had already established a connection with the IHR, founded in 1921. A complete set of volumes was presented to the Institute in 1922, and Page was given a room in the building. In 1932 he proposed to the Director of the IHR, A.F. Pollard, that he should give the VCH to the Institute on his death. The transaction was completed quite quickly and Page donated to the University all the stock in hand of all volumes in the VCH already published and the copyrights connected with these: all manuscripts and drafts already prepared for further volumes and the connected copyrights; the library of books and other material collected for future volumes, including notes, maps and plans; and all contracts both for the publication and sale of the work, and with subscribers. Page was to have the use of the library in his lifetime.

The transfer took place in 1933, when the University of London passed management of the VCH to the IHR. By the time the transfer was finished in February 1933, 92 volumes had appeared, and ten counties had been completed. It had become largely associated with the Home Counties and the rural heartlands of central England.

The hope of covering Wales, and even Monmouth, was abandoned in the 1920s, and the extremities and the maritime counties were virtually untouched territory. Northumberland had also been given up.

As The Times noted 'All who know the value of that great but still far from finished work, the Victoria County History, will be glad to learn that it is henceforth to be produced under the auspices of the University of London'. 'Its future', the newspaper added, 'is not only assured, but lies in the hands of one of the few bodies really competent to undertake it'. Both parties accepted that the university was not obliged to continue the VCH, though it has done so for almost 80 years.

The history of the years 1933–1990 is told in the General Introduction (1970) and its Supplement (1991). Recent developments are recorded in the The Little Big Red Book (2008). A summary can also be found at www.victoriacountyhistory.ac.uk.

THE ARCHIVES

The VCH began life as a private enterprise run by the publishers Archibald Constable & Co., from their premises at 2 Whitehall Gardens (now demolished). With the appointment in 1904 of William Page as sole editor (he had been acting jointly with the first editor, H.A. Doubleday, 1902–4) the office was moved to more spacious premises on James (now Orange) Street near the National Portrait Gallery. The building has been demolished. All the VCH archival material was collected at Orange Street. It included the voluminous correspondence from editors, contributors and committee members around the country, much of it prior to late 1908. It also includes copy out-letters from

General volumes of 1901 (Norfolk I) and 1906 (Devon I) in their original binding.

Doubleday's time in bound volumes, now boxes A21–A28 at the IHR, and in envelopes (together with the originals) from Page's period as General Editor (boxes A29–A58).

The majority of the archive consisted of slips and draft manorial descents. The early VCH employed staff to sift the published and unpublished indexes available in the Public Record Office, British Museum and Lambeth Palace Library, for references on a parish-by-parish basis nationwide. Each reference was recorded on a single piece of paper (a slip) and these were collated by county, hundred and parish. They were stored by county. Additionally, for some counties manorial descents and other unpublished material also survives in the archive. A great deal of work drafted before 1908 was never published in the case of counties for which no funds were available after 1910.

When a county was completed, it was not always clear what fate should befall the slips. For Hampshire they are now to be found in Southampton University Library. Occasionally slips seem to have been sent to working County Editors, and not necessarily returned. All the slips for Cumberland are in Carlisle Library, where they have been since the death of Revd James Wilson in 1923. Material for Cornwall is now in the Royal Institute library, Truro.

When work on the VCH resumed following the First World War, Page was guardian of the whole archive. In 1922 he moved to Sussex and built a 'storehouse' for the accumulated material, estimated at the time to weigh 14 tons. In 1933, when the University of London took over the VCH, it acquired the complete archive, which was stored initially at the School of Hygiene, Malet Street. At some point, possibly in the war, the majority of the archive was moved out of London to an abandoned church in Northamptonshire. It was recovered only in 1947.

By this time, the VCH was expanding out of London into the counties, and this is reflected in the way that correspondence was archived, by county and time period in the 'B', 'Q' and 'R' series in the IHR. To facilitate the work of county-based staff, the appropriate slips were moved to the county office. When volumes were published, the slips associated with a particular hundred were usually deposited in the local record office. For counties where no work was in progress, the slips were moved to the University of London's outstore at Egham (part of the Royal Holloway complex), from which they could be called up to London if needed.

In 2007 it was decided by the VCH National Committee to offer the slips to local record offices, whether or not a particular county was 'active'. As a result, the majority of slips have now been moved out of Egham, and deposited locally. The VCH Central Office's archive material is at Senate House, and active counties maintain their own archives (including their slips).

SELECT BIBLIOGRAPHY

General Introductions

R.B. Pugh (ed.), The Victoria History of the Counties of England. General Introduction (Oxford, 1970) 1–27.

C.R. Elrington (ed.), The Victoria History of the Counties of England. General Introduction: Supplement 1970–90 (Oxford, 1990) 1–8.

K. Whitston and M. Hackett (eds), The Little Big Red Book (2008)

Recent articles on the VCH and its counties by John Beckett

'The Thoroton Society and the VCH', Trans. of the Thoroton Soc., 113 (2009), 119–36

'W.G. Hoskins, the VCH, and the Study of English Local History', Midland Hist., 36/1 (2011), 115–27

with Charles Watkins, 'Natural History and local history in late Victorian and Edwardian England: the contribution of the VCH', Rural Hist., 22/1 (2011), 59–87.

'Topography and landscape history: the role of the VCH', Landscape Hist., 32/2 (2011), 57–65

'The VCH in Devon, 1899–1910', Rpt and Trans. of the Devonshire Assocn, 143 (2011), 283–310

'Canon Thomas Taylor of St Just and the VCH in Cornwall, 1899–1938', Jnl of the Royal Instn of Cornwall, (2011), 31–44

'W.G. Hoskins and the VCH in Leicestershire', Trans. of the Leics. Archaeol. and Hist. Soc. 85 (2011), 165–91

'The Cumberland and Westmorland Antiquarian and Archaeological Society and the VCH', Trans. of the Cumberland and Westmorland Antiqu. and Archaeol. Soc. (2011), 207–25

THE COUNTIES

BEDFORDSHIRE

Bedfordshire is one of England's smallest counties, yet because it lies on the routes north from London, it is crossed by three mainline railways and both the A1 and M1. Its gentle landscape stretches from the Chiltern Hills at its southernmost tip to the clay belt north of Bedford, dominated until recently by the tall chimneys of numerous brickworks. But Bedfordshire also has notable country houses — Luton Hoo, Wrest Park and Woburn Abbey — as well as two huge airship hangars at Cardington, built two years after the three volumes of the VCH *Bedfordshire* set were completed in 1914. Only one general volume was published, in 1904, with sections on geology and natural history as well as prehistory, Anglo-Saxon archaeology, Domesday, ecclesiastical history, and religious houses. Today the histories of parishes in Bedfordshire's nine hundreds, covered in volumes II and III, would benefit from being developed to include newly available information.

BERKSHIRE

The VCH account of the historic county was completed in four volumes between 1906 and 1924, with an index published in 1927. Two cover general topics to the standard plan, while another two chart the parishes of Berkshire's 20 hundreds. The sections on borough government are still considered useful despite being written over 90 years ago. Of the county's boroughs Windsor is famous not only for its town but for the royal castle, illustrated by a coloured fold-out plan by Sir W.S. St John Hope, author in 1913 of the castle's official history. In the late 20th century, industries associated with information technology were established along the M4 in England's 'Silicon Valley'. This and the huge changes to Reading, Maidenhead and other towns mean that another volume would be a welcome addition to the history of what has been, since 1957, the Royal County of Berkshire.

BUCKINGHAMSHIRE

Buckinghamshire has a diverse landscape including the Chiltern Hills, Thames valley and vale of Aylesbury. Work was begun to the standard plan of four volumes just before 1914; the last volume was published in 1927, an index in 1928. The enterprise was supervised by the Buckinghamshire County Committee, chaired by the Hon. Walter Rothschild, MP for Aylesbury 1899–1910. In common with most general volumes of this period, there is a substantial article on natural history, with sections on palaeontology, molluscs, spiders and crustaceans by regular VCH contributors, including Revd T.R.R. Stebbing. The histories of the parishes in Buckinghamshire's 18 hundreds have good accounts of manors and parish churches, and the changes caused by arrival of the

Metropolitan railway are well observed. More on London's influence, the development of RAF Air Command at Naphill near High Wycombe, and the absorption of many parishes into Milton Keynes would make worthwhile additions to the story.

CAMBRIDGESHIRE & THE ISLE OF ELY

Although research into Cambridgeshire began in the early years of the 20th century, alongside work on neighbouring counties Bedfordshire and Hertfordshire, nothing was published. The series was revived in the inter-war years when the project was taken over by the University of London. L.F. Salzman, third General Editor, produced general volumes in 1938 and 1948 before work began on the parishes of Cambridgeshire's 17 hundreds. Those histories were among the first to benefit from the wider range of subjects tackled by the VCH. Volumes were dedicated to the county's two major historic towns: *Cambridge* (II, 1959) and the *City of Ely* (IV, 1953). The project was run from the IHR until the set was completed with the publication of volume X in 2002. The parish histories do justice to the unusual landscape of chalk plain, claylands and fen and to a rich medieval and institutional history; consequently there are no plans to update the set.

CHESHIRE

Except towards Manchester and the Mersey, the County Palatine of Chester is mainly rural. In 1972 it was one of only four counties which had no VCH volume, but in that year the Cheshire VCH was established, with support from the Leverhulme Trust, Cheshire County Council, and Liverpool University. It made swift progress with general articles published in three volumes between 1979 and 1987. Although no progress was made on the parishes of 11 of the 12 Domesday hundreds, the City of Chester was investigated in detail in a volume published in two parts in 2002 and 2005: it was edited by C.P. Lewis and A.T. Thacker, who refined the established formula for VCH urban studies in which a chronological account is accompanied by sections on particular topics. Despite much local interest, particularly from the Cheshire and Chester Archives Service, no substantial funding has been forthcoming to continue work in county.

DEVONSHIRE

The first volume of *VCH Devon*, published in 1906, was mainly concerned with natural history, with some material on Anglo-Saxon remains, Domesday, feudal baronage and ancient earthworks. There is much for the VCH to do: Devon is one of the largest English counties, with 38 hundreds recorded at the time of Domesday. Most of Devon has a notably beautiful landscape. It shares with Dorset the Jurassic Coast, England's only natural UNESCO World Heritage Site, and with Somerset the Exmoor National Park, in addition to its own Dartmoor. There is a rich history of fishing and naval activity along the picturesque north and south coastlines, and the county town of Exeter has a magnificent cathedral and many medieval buildings. Although no topographical volumes have appeared, between 2005 and 2009 the parishes of West Ansty, East Ansty, Molland and Twitchen were included in the EPE Exmoor project, and in the associated paperback, *Exmoor: The Making of an English Upland* (2009).

DORSET

Like neighbouring Devon, Dorset lacks any topographical volumes, but does have two general volumes. Confusingly the first to be published was the second of the four planned volumes. It appeared in 1908 and covered the ecclesiastical history of the county. The next to be published, 60 years later, was edited by the VCH General Editor, R.B. Pugh, and covers the Dorset sections of the Domesday Book and Geld Rolls. Volume I of the series was never completed, and consequently there is no VCH account of Dorset's natural history or of the county's rich archaeological record, including Iron Age hill forts such as Maiden Castle, and extensive Roman remains at Dorchester. A regional approach to research could help the VCH to make a start on recording the history of the many parishes of both Dorset and Devon.

HERTFORDSHIRE

Despite much of Hertfordshire forming part of the London commuter belt, the county retains the largely agrarian character which has shaped its landscape and economy since the Iron Age. Recorded at the time of Domesday as having nine hundreds, Hertfordshire has a rich historic environment with Norman castles at Berkhampstead and Bishops Stortford, and notable archaeological remains especially from the Roman occupation: Icknield way, Ermine and Watling streets passed through the county, the last linking Verulamium (now the cathedral city of St Albans) to London. *VCH Hertfordshire* was completed in four volumes between 1902 and 1914 by the General Editor, William Page, who lived in St Albans from 1896; an index appeared in 1923. Because so much has changed, the series could be expanded to reflect new archaeological excavation, developments such as the rise of aircraft manufacturing, construction of several new towns, decline in brewing, and the importance of Elstree in the television and film industries.

HUNTINGDONSHIRE

Huntingdonshire, originally planned to be two volumes, was published in three volumes between 1926 and 1938, underwritten by Grenville Proby. Work was then restarted in 1924. Some of the general articles were re-worked pre-First World War contributions which had not been published (for example, the natural history sections in volume I) and some were specially commissioned for the volume. The topographical entries in volumes two and three were mainly reworked versions of material prepared in the VCH London office before 1910. An index volume was published in 1938.

LANCASHIRE

The completion of *VCH Lancashire* in eight volumes between 1906 and 1914 singles out Lancashire as the most productive VCH county prior to the outbreak of the First World War. That the set was completed so expeditiously was due to the tireless efforts of Dr William Farrer, a retired textiles manufacturer who, after his retirement in 1897, began working to complete a new history of Lancashire upon the lines of R.W. Eyton's

Antiquities of Shropshire. Despite Farrer's dedication, he might never have finished his history had he not joined forces with the VCH's promoters. Farrer was assisted by John Brownhill in compiling the parish histories for Lancashire's six hundreds, with other contributors for the two general volumes, and produced a volume a year. The whole Lancashire set is still available to buy. A useful addition to it would be new studies of urban development, for example of Liverpool where an EPE paperback planned for publication in 2013–14 as an outcome of a major research project.

LINCOLNSHIRE

England's second largest county remains one of the VCH's greatest challenges. Only one general volume was produced: volume I on natural history was never completed, but volume II of the set was published in 1906. Now over a century old, it has in many respects never been replaced as a work of reference. It begins with the county's ecclesiastical history, with entries for each religious house, and continues with chapters on political history, social and economic history (including a table summarising the first 11 national censuses), industries, agriculture, forestry, endowed schools, and sport. Although further research was carried out, mainly by W.O. Massingbird, it was never published, and so the task of writing every parish history is still to be done. The county town of Lincoln, with its castle, cathedral and late-medieval timber-framed buildings, would make a fine VCH urban study in the style of that produced for Chester.

NORFOLK

The first volume of the Norfolk series, covering natural history, was published in 1901; it was the third of all VCH volumes to be produced since its founding in 1899. Edited by H. Arthur Doubleday, it was followed in 1906 by volume II, edited by William Page, who included chapters on Domesday, Danegeld, ecclesiastical history, religious houses, medieval painting and early Christian art. No progress was made on histories of Norfolk's 36 Domesday hundreds, and at present there is no VCH work taking place in the county. However, there is an extremely strong appetite for local history within the county, which has a network of lively historical and archaeological societies and a Centre for East Anglian Studies within the University of East Anglia. With the Centre as a supporter of the VCH, it is hoped that work may begin soon on researching parish histories.

NORTHUMBERLAND

Northumberland is known worldwide for Hadrian's Wall, and for a string of castles at Alnwick, Bamburgh, Dunstanburgh, Lindisfarne, Newcastle and Warkworth which testify to the tumultuous history of this frontier county. But despite the richness of its history, Northumberland remains the only English county for which no VCH work has ever taken place. The explanation lies in the existence of numerous other accounts of the county's history, most significant of which is *A History of Northumberland*, issued in 11 volumes by the Northumberland County History Committee between 1893 and 1940. It records the parishes of Northumberland's six hundreds in much the same way as the VCH has done for other counties. A VCH series would be a duplication of effort, but although there are no plans to begin work in the county, there is scope for the VCH to produce studies of the general topics usually included in a Victoria County History.

RUTLAND

Rutland is the smallest of the historic English counties and has only two towns, Oakham and Uppingham. So small is it that one general volume (1908), and one topographical volume (1935) were all that was required to cover the county. In 1974, Rutland ceased to exist as an independent county, and its villages and towns were transferred to Leicestershire. But in 1997 after two decades of local campaigning, Rutland was recognised as an independent unitary authority, the smallest in England, and as a postal county by the Royal Mail in 2007. Rutland's inhabitants are fiercely proud of its identity, and its history is actively promoted by the Rutland Local History and Record Society.

SUFFOLK

The story of VCH Suffolk shares many similarities with VCH Norfolk. Two general volumes, edited by Page, were published out of sequence in 1907 and 1911, with volume II covering the religious houses including St Edmunds abbey, followed by volume I on natural history. Despite the guidance of a county committee, established in 1907 and comprising local nobility, gentry, mayors, clergy and historians, no work took place after 1918. In 2009, a meeting was held to discuss restarting research into parish and town histories but, although enthusiasm remains high in the county, a practical plan awaits development. In addition to writing Suffolk's parish histories, it would be valuable to examine the county's archaeological record, rich in finds and sites from the Stone, Bronze and Iron ages and in Anglo-Saxon evidence, among which is the famous treasure from Sutton Hoo, part of a ship burial of international significance discovered in 1939.

SURREY

VCH Surrey was completed to the standard plan of two general and two topographical volumes between 1902 and 1912, followed in 1914 by an index. With Bedfordshire and Hampshire, it was one of the first county sets to be completed. Surrey has a well-established local history community and an excellent county archive at the Surrey History Centre, and there is significant scope to add to the VCH history with an account of the county in the 20th century, a period which saw the spread of London to include Croydon, the dramatic growth of Guildford and Farnham and the planned expansion of Redhill, and the construction of Sir Edward Maufe's Guildford cathedral. The inter-war years also saw Brooklands near Weybridge become a centre for motorsport.

WARWICKSHIRE

Warwickshire has a complete county set, its last volume having been published in 1969. Work began in 1904 and 1908 with two volumes on the standard topics of natural history, Domesday, ecclesiastical history and religious houses, but then stalled. The appointment of Philip Styles as part-time local editor, two years after the VCH had restarted in 1935, led to the first topographical volume, on Barlichway Hundred, appearing in 1945. Between 1945 and 1951, parishes in Warwickshire's three remaining hundreds appeared in three further volumes, all noted for good coverage of vernacular buildings; an index followed in 1955. The major urban centres, Birmingham in volume VII and Coventry and the borough of Warwick in volume VIII, completed the set. Most of the history, in VCH terms, is quite recent with detailed treatment and a wide range of topics; consequently, there are no plans to update it, although interest has been shown in producing an expanded account of the city of Birmingham.

WORCESTERSHIRE

Worcestershire is the only West Midlands county for which a complete VCH history was produced before 1930: it was covered in four volumes, plus an index, between 1901 and 1926. Although much of the research and writing for the last two volumes had been completed by 1915, publication was delayed by the war. All five books were edited or co-edited by John William Willis-Bund, a local lawyer, historian and politician, who was awarded a CBE in 1918 and appointed Vice-Lieutenant of Worcestershire in 1924. A predominantly rural county, known for fruit production now restricted to the area around the Vale of Evesham, the major centres are the cathedral city of Worcester, the towns of Bromsgrove, Stourport-on-Severn, Droitwich, Evesham, Kidderminster, Malvern, and the largest place, Redditch. In 1974 Worcestershire was merged with neighbouring Herefordshire to form the county of Hereford and Worcester, although it regained its independence in 1998. After nearly a century since the first volumes appeared there is clearly scope to add to the VCH history.

YORKSHIRE

In its treatment of the county of Yorkshire, the largest in the United Kingdom, the VCH planned to compile topographical accounts in accordance with Yorkshire's ancient division into three ridings — North, East and West — and to treat the county as a whole for general subjects. The first three volumes, which were edited by William Page and published between 1907 and 1913, covered the standard topics including natural history, ancient earthworks, Anglo-Saxon remains, Domesday, ecclesiastical history and religious houses. The three ridings were abolished in 1974 when Yorkshire was reorganised into non-metropolitan counties but the VCH has kept to the historic organisation of the county's ridings, themselves divided into wapentakes which in Yorkshire take the place of hundreds as the main administrative units. Yorkshire North Riding has been completed, the East Riding makes good progress (*see below*), but the largest of the ridings, the West Riding has only recently been started.

YORKSHIRE NORTH RIDING

The North Riding's parishes, in 12 wapentakes, were covered in two fat volumes, edited by Page; their publication in 1914 and 1923 followed hot on the heels of the general county volumes. In his own guide to the riding published in 1966, Sir Nikolaus Pevsner acknowledged that 'It was a great help that the Victoria County History has done the whole of the North Riding, and with the principal architectural descriptions [of sites including Richmond Castle, Castle Howard and Rievaulx Abbey] by such men as Sir Charles Peers, Sir W.H. St John Hope, and Sir Alfred Clapham.' The contents page which lists the contributions made by those scholars and many others, illustrates the huge undertaking shouldered by Page in the early years.

YORKSHIRE: CITY OF YORK

The VCH restarted work in Yorkshire in 1950. The first publication, in 1961, was a single volume on the City of York, which was independent of the ridings. It is organised like subsequent VCH urban histories into a series of chronological chapters, and a second part covering particular topics such as the King's Manor, the city walls and places of entertainment.

YORKSHIRE WEST RIDING

There are stark differences between the north and south of the county. The southern part became a centre of industrial production: Leeds, Huddersfield, Halifax, Dewsbury, Bradford, and Saltaire (a World Heritage Site) are all associated with the woollen industry, Sheffield with steel production and cutlery making, and Barnsley with coal mining, while Doncaster is the home of GNR locomotive engineering. In contrast, the northern region remains mostly rural, and includes the dramatic landscapes of the Yorkshire Dales National Park which straddles the boundary between the West and North Ridings. The richness of the history and topography has proved a challenge to the VCH. Until 2009 not a single parish history had been started, but in that year Dr Brodie Waddell, funded by a generous bequest from Rena Fenteman to compile a history of Barlow, the village of her ancestors, produced the first VCH parish account for the West Riding. It can be read on the VCH website, and we hope it will provide the catalyst for further work.

CORNWALL

Work to seek support, subscriptions and contributions began in Cornwall in 1901. Research and writing started in the following year, and a general history volume was published in 1906. Although more work was done in the 1920s, no more volumes were published. It was not until 2010 that volume II (*Religious History to 1560*) appeared, thanks to its author Professor Nicholas Orme.

The invitation to participate in a national VCH scheme for 'dormant' counties, partly funded by the HLF, but with substantial local contributions, offered an opportunity for Cornwall to re-establish its VCH more securely.

Following the successful completion of that project, with publication of paperbacks on Cornish Christianity and the Cornish coast (see p. 96), a newly-formed charitable Trust identified its aim as continuing to explore, with volunteer and professional help, ways of investigating the history of Cornish communities to national VCH standards.

Three teams of volunteers are working on a range of documentary sources to develop a template for a standard approach to the collection, recording and dissemination of information which can be used in future VCH publications. Essential partners are the Cornwall Record Office and Cornish Studies Library (www.cornwall.gov.uk) which provide training in the use of sources, and the department of history at the University of Exeter, Tremough Campus, Cornwall (www.exeter.ac.uk/cornwall).

Members of the Launceston group inspecting and discussing a historical map of the county (image courtesy of VCH Cornwall).

Cornwall's landscape has over centuries been transformed by industrial development and much has been written about the county's mining heritage, now awarded the status of a World Heritage Site. But what was life like before the development of local industry? One area currently under investigation is the group of parishes around St Austell in mid-Cornwall, with its unique post-industrial 'moonscape' of clay tips and deep lagoons. It was here, in 1763, that William Cookworthy discovered the fine clay with which to make porcelain: what impact did this have on the people living there — farmers and tinners — and on an agricultural and moorland landscape?

Characteristic too are the 21 little towns which were formerly important Parliamentary boroughs: how did the loss of status and privilege affect them and the people who lived there? Work on the former boroughs of Grampound (very rotten, disenfranchised in 1830) and Launceston, 'gateway to Cornwall', which retained its Parliamentary representation until 1885, is revealing very different kinds of communities.

The documents now being used include probate records, maps and plans, leases and other property documents, as well as parish registers. Those records are common to many parishes, capable of standardised recording of the information in them, and for the period being studied *c.*1750–1850, not too difficult for volunteers to read and understand; they are though only a small selection from Cornwall's archival heritage. Standard guidelines are being developed for recording and making available the information collected by the teams, with regular training days, discussion sessions, and the experimental use of computerised mapping and indexing systems. Transcripts of 500 wills across seven parishes are already on the VCH website.

Informative displays are mounted at fundraising events and at local venues, to inform and enthuse the people whose communities we are studying. We have had a stand at the Royal Cornwall Show (regular attendance over 120,000) each year since 2002; this year the Show will be at the end of the Diamond Jubilee week — a real chance to celebrate our achievements so far.

An exciting new venture is the plan to publish work in progress in e-book form, initially featuring profiles of families and farms in the 'clay' parish of St Stephen in Brannel. We will also expand work in Launceston towards a history of the town and its three parishes.

Our aim is to develop and refine our pilot scheme and to extend it back through time and county-wide, 'turning back the layers' of Cornwall's history through the study of its documents, buildings and landscape.

So far what we have achieved has been with minimal funding, and with many volunteers refusing to accept any reimbursement, even for travelling, in this very rural county. Although Cornwall is not a rich county it has already raised over £70,000 towards the completion of the Lottery-supported project. The trustees are determined that once awakened, VCH Cornwall will not again slumber for another 100 years.

ELAINE HENDERSON - ADMINISTRATOR
LADY BANHAM - CHAIR OF TRUST

www.victoriacountyhistory.ac.uk/counties/cornwall

CUMBRIA

Although VCH Cumberland was started with two general volumes, no topographical volumes have been published for the historic counties of Cumberland and Westmorland; the only parts of Cumbria to have been researched in detail by the VCH are the Furness and Cartmel areas, which were formerly in Lancashire and are covered in *VCH Lancashire* VIII (1910). So, for the bulk of the county, the VCH Cumbria project, launched in 2010, is starting from scratch. Working with volunteers, we have embarked on a programme to start the process of researching and writing parish histories for Cumberland and Westmorland.

The project is being organised by the Cumbria County History Trust, a charitable association established in 2010 to further the VCH. Trustees include representatives of a wide range of bodies interested in promoting history and heritage in Cumbria. The Trust has already succeeded in raising enough from subscriptions and local sources to employ a Volunteer Coordinator on a part-time basis, and to mount a programme of tailor-made training events for VCH volunteers in Cumbria.

The project is run from the Department of History at Lancaster University, under the direction of Professor Angus Winchester, who is acting as County Editor, and the Volunteer Coordinator, Dr Sarah Rose.

Individuals from the local history community in Cumbria responded to a call for volunteers to undertake research for the VCH. Guided by the Volunteer Coordinator, they have embarked on essential groundwork for the project. Initial tasks included compiling population figures for every parish and township in Cumberland and Westmorland from 1801 to 2001; preparing bibliographies of published work on individual places; and undertaking preliminary research. Since summer 2011, a smaller core of volunteers has started detailed research on a number of parishes to make a start on drafting full VCH parish histories.

We are marking the Jubilee by preparing brief digests of historical data for every community in Cumbria, to provide county-wide coverage of historical data at a basic level, on which future work towards VCH parish histories can build. Key data on administrative status, acreage, population, landholding, economic activity, places of worship and schools will be included. Volunteers are undertaking a structured programme of research in key sources to compile these digests, which will be posted on the project website. This work builds on the substantial progress already made in gathering basic data about parishes throughout Cumberland and Westmorland.

Volunteers, working as individuals or in small teams under the close supervision of the County Editor, have embarked on researching and writing the first tranche of parish histories. Work is actively underway on eight parishes, scattered across Cumbria: Stanwix and Kirkandrews upon Esk in the far north of the county; Addingham and Renwick in eastern Cumberland; Papcastle, near Cockermouth; Brough under Stainmore in north-east Westmorland; and Kirkby Lonsdale and Skelsmergh in the south. As drafts are completed, these will be posted on the project website while volunteers move on to research further parishes.

VCH Cumbria volunteers. One of the regular round-table meetings with volunteers to discuss their work and give guidance on researching and writing parish histories (image courtesy of VCH Cumbria).

The project website (www.cumbriacountyhistory.org.uk) is both the gateway to training materials and resources for volunteers, and the repository of completed work. It is rapidly becoming a valuable resource for local historians in Cumbria, providing access to:

- Full census data for the parishes and townships in Cumberland and Westmorland from 1801 to 2001 (already posted)
- Digests of historical data for every community in Cumbria (being compiled during 2012)
- Draft parish histories as these are completed
- Other research materials generated by the project.

ANGUS WINCHESTER - COUNTY EDITOR
BRYAN GRAY CBE - CHAIR OF TRUST

www.victoriacountyhistory.ac.uk/counties/cumberland
www.cumbriacountyhistory.org.uk

DERBYSHIRE

The early history of VCH in Derbyshire followed much the same course as in most counties. Two general volumes, arranged on standard lines, appeared in 1905 and 1907, the first notable for a Domesday text edited by a young F.M. Stenton in one of his earliest pieces of published work, rather than J.H. Round, who wrote most of the Domesday sections in those years. Thousands of slips were made for topographical volumes, of which none were published before work came to a halt shortly before the First World War, although considerable progress was made on parish histories for Appletree hundred (alphabetically the first in the county), including draft text. This was the work of Cicely Wilmot, one of the young women then working for VCH who had completed the Oxford final honours school of modern history but could not be admitted to a degree. Miss Wilmot was a distant member of the Chaddesden branch of the Wilmot family and thus had easy access to the gentry of south-west Derbyshire, from whom she was able to collect information at first hand.

The early demise of VCH in Derbyshire appears to have aroused no comment locally. An attempt to revive the project during the optimistic years after 1945 made no progress, and only one passing reference to such a scheme occurred in the 1980s.

The modern history of VCH in Derbyshire begins with the Act amending the law relating to the National Lottery, which appeared to open the way to support for VCH in any county where matching funds could be raised. Thus encouraged, the Derbyshire Archaeological Society, Derbyshire Record Society and Derbyshire Family History

The south front of Chatsworth House (1688–1694), designed for the 1st Duke of Devonshire by William Talman, the leading court architect of his day (photo reproduced by permission of Chatsworth House Trust).

Society issued a joint appeal to their members which met with a gratifying response. This appeal was aimed at raising small, regular contributions (generally £5 a month) from as many people as possible, who would make up a voluntary association of individuals, the Derbyshire VCH Trust. The original target of 200 members has never quite been achieved, but those who have joined the trust have been extraordinarily loyal over a long period. While the negotiations with the HLF were continuing, the Derbyshire Trust decided to make a start on work in the county. Helped by the Derbyshire Library Service, whose local studies staff have been indefatigable supporters of VCH, and by the University of Nottingham, whose History Department agreed to provide facilities (and later a post) for a part-time County Editor, work began in 2002 on a topographical volume on the north-east of the county. At the same time, trust members were encouraged to become actively involved by joining groups in different parts of the county, organised on the lines of traditional university continuing education classes, and material was collected (and some text drafted) for other parishes.

Between 2005 and 2009 Derbyshire took part in the England's Past for Everyone project, the eventual outcome of the application to the HLF. Two attractively produced paperbacks, one on Bolsover and the other on the Hardwick Hall estate, emerged from this work. After EPE came to an end, work resumed on a hardback volume covering Bolsover and four adjoining communities, all dominated in recent times by the coal mining industry (Barlborough, Clowne, Creswell and Whitwell), which is scheduled for publication in 2013.

Over the last decade a good deal has been achieved in Derbyshire. If the present level of support from trust members, Nottingham University and Derbyshire County Council can be sustained, the completion of further hardback volumes, for which a great deal of material has already been collected, should accelerate. Even if progress has been slower than many would have wished, the fact that work on VCH has been started and sustained in a county with a weak tradition of interest in local history is something which all concerned can be proud of.

DUKE OF DEVONSHIRE KCVO, CBE, DL
PRESIDENT, DERBYSHIRE VCH TRUST

PHILIP RIDEN - COUNTY EDITOR

www.victoriacountyhistory.ac.uk/counties/derbyshire

DURHAM

Three volumes, including one on topography, had been published by 1928, but since the Durham VCH was revived in 1999, the history of the county has been steadily enhanced. Volume IV of the county history, on Darlington, was published in 2005, and volume V (Sunderland) is in progress. Three paperbacks (one on Darlington and two on Sunderland) have been produced.

Durham was chosen as one of the pilots for Heritage Lottery funding, later England's Past for Everyone, so was already running when the main funding came on stream. It pioneered many of the new approaches which EPE ushered in, including use of volunteers, engagement with the local community, and online dissemination. For a while university-based (Durham, Sunderland, Teesside, at various times), Durham VCH always ran independently of the county council. Since funding for full-time staff ended in 2009, the current project — the history of Sunderland — has been carried forward by a consultant County Editor and freelance writers, supported by a grant from the Marc Fitch Fund. The Sunderland volume is scheduled for publication in 2013/14.

The Durham VCH Trust continues its work thanks to the dedication and support of its subscribers and occasional donors. The Trust committee, largely a professional body of historians and archivists, has a hands-on approach. It is not cash-rich, so the future lies with volunteers. One team has been working for many years on probate and related sources for the east of the county, contributing significantly to the history of Sunderland and continuing into the neighbouring parish of Easington.

A significant achievement of this group was the publication by the Surtees Society, the leading record society of the north-east of England, of transcripts of *Sunderland Wills and Inventories, 1601–50* (2010). We hope to build on this volunteer endeavour and move forward to a full history of Easington parish.

Volunteers are also to be at the centre of a forthcoming preliminary survey for a history of the ancient parish of Gainford, which will have as its starting point the unpublished draft of the parish history completed a century ago. 'Pump priming' funding for this has come through the HLF-supported Heart of Teesdale project. The early-20th century proof will be made available on line, with an explanatory preface, and in association with the three principal local history societies we will undertake a feasibility study for a full new history. We envisage this model of partnership as a way ahead for Durham. The Gainford project also represents a move away from the predominantly urban and industrial focus of volumes IV and V, to the mainly rural and agricultural societies of the west of the county. A study in Teesdale means that records of great lay landholders will be explored on a more significant scale, as well as the county's rich ecclesiastical documentation and more modern records associated with coal-mining and heavy industry which have been extensively used in our recent work in the two urban centres.

GILLIAN COOKSON - CONSULTANT EDITOR, ANTHONY POLLARD - CHAIR OF TRUST

www.victoriacountyhistory.ac.uk/counties/durham

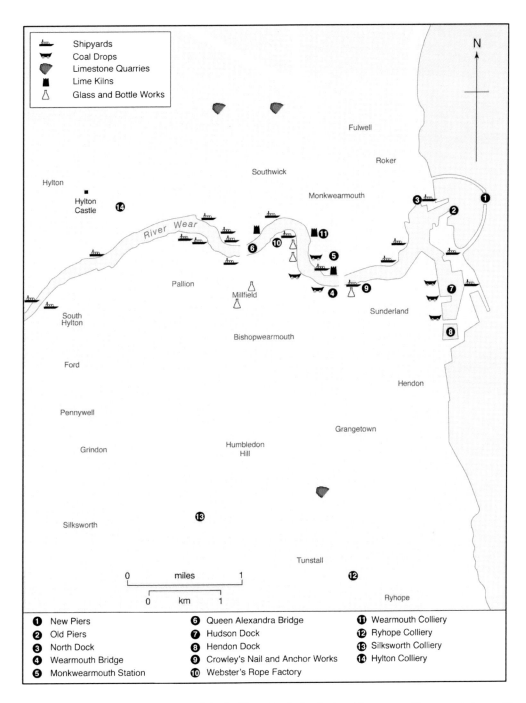

Legend

- Shipyards
- Coal Drops
- Limestone Quarries
- Lime Kilns
- Glass and Bottle Works

N

Fulwell

Roker

Hylton

Southwick

Hylton Castle

Monkwearmouth

River Wear

Pallion

Millfield

Sunderland

South Hylton

Bishopwearmouth

Hendon

Ford

Pennywell

Grangetown

Grindon

Humbledon Hill

Silksworth

Tunstall

Ryhope

miles 0 1

km 0 1

❶ New Piers	❻ Queen Alexandra Bridge	⓫ Wearmouth Colliery
❷ Old Piers	❼ Hudson Dock	⓬ Ryhope Colliery
❸ North Dock	❽ Hendon Dock	⓭ Silksworth Colliery
❹ Wearmouth Bridge	❾ Crowley's Nail and Anchor Works	⓮ Hylton Colliery
❺ Monkwearmouth Station	❿ Webster's Rope Factory	

Although best known for coal mining and shipbuilding. Sunderland's riverside communities supported a wealth of industries in the 19th century. Sunderland's collieries, shipyards, lime kilns, bottleworks and quarries, along with bridges and docks, are here marked on a modern base map first published in Sunderland: Building a City. *For a full account of Sunderland's industry see the forthcoming* VCH Durham V.

ESSEX

Essex is a large county encompassing tracts of unspoilt countryside and many small attractive market towns as well as substantial urban and industrial developments. The disparaging epithet 'flat Essex' hardly reflects the county's extremely varied landscape and, as Nikolaus Pevsner commented in 1954, it deserves to be better known for 'touring and sight-seeing'. Among its virtues are a rich architectural heritage in medieval churches and vernacular timber-framed buildings, many of the finest being associated with the wealth generated by the cloth industry. The lengthy coastline, indented by river estuaries and creeks, also has a fascinating past through its many industries (for example, salt, fishing, oysters), its trading links with London and the Continent, its seaside resorts, and its military defences.

Until the start of the VCH Essex series in 1903 the most complete county history remained Revd Philip Morant's History and Antiquities of the County of Essex (1768). After a second general volume (1907) the VCH series lapsed until 1951 when it was revived by a committee financed by the local authorities in association with the University of London. Since then a further nine volumes (one on Roman Essex and eight topographical volumes) have been produced, plus three bibliographical volumes (unique to Essex). Volumes IV–VIII cover the topography of south-west Essex, including the London boroughs east of the river Lea, Harlow and Ongar. Volumes IX and X cover the borough of Colchester and surrounding parishes including many in 'Constable country' along the Stour valley, while volume XI studies the north-east Essex seaside resorts. Volume XII will be a topographical volume concerned with mainly rural parishes in north-east Essex.

Research has benefited from the exceptional quality of Essex parish and manorial archives, mainly a by-product of the early establishment of the Essex Record Office (ERO) in 1938. VCH volumes are available in the ERO and in all Essex public libraries, but as research is completed draft texts are now also placed on our website. Electronic copies of volumes two and four to ten of the series are available free via British History Online (www.british-history.ac.uk). The Essex volumes receive an average of over 200,000 'hits' annually, reflecting high demand from people all over the world who have Essex connections.

Essex has led the way with the development of VCH volunteering. Independent researchers with academic qualifications have contributed to many articles in VCH Essex volumes. The members of the Clacton VCH Group (founded 2002) have concentrated on the history of the Second World War and produced successful events, displays and publications for the general public and school pupils. The group now plans to assist the VCH by studying coastal landing places in north-east Essex. The Newport Victoria County History Group has been researching Newport in north-west Essex to produce a VCH parish history, while other volunteers are exploring a possible new project on the history of Southend-on-Sea. Ultimately, the extension of VCH coverage over the remainder of the county may depend upon the wider use of such volunteers.

The VCH Essex Trust was formed in 1994 and, since direct local government funding ceased at the end of 2010, it now finances the project and employs editors as contractors.

Paycocke's House in Coggeshall, now in the care of The National Trust, showing the five-bay façade with oriel windows, and richly carved bressumer that bears the initials and merchant's mark of the clothier Thomas Paycocke. Although heavily restored it is one of the most attractive timber-framed buildings in England. Recent work commissioned by The National Trust combined architectural analysis, tree-ring dating and documentary research (the latter undertaken by VCH Essex County Editor) to confirm that it was built by Paycocke and his wife Margaret Horrold, a wealthy heiress from a Suffolk clothier family, in 1509–10 (image courtesy of James Butler).

Office facilities are provided by Essex County Council at the Essex Record Office. That the trustees and members decided to continue not only demonstrates their commitment to the VCH but also their understanding that, in order to reap the full benefits of the very large public investment made so far, the series needs to be completed. The Trust holds an AGM and public lecture and produces a newsletter *Essex Past*. In October 2011 it held an event to celebrate the 60th anniversary of the revived Essex project and to launch a new fundraising drive. The Trust has been supported by generous donations from individuals and from many other local trusts and societies who represent tens of thousands of Essex people who are directly or indirectly benefited by the VCH project.

To find out more about VCH Essex, or make a contribution to our fundraising, please visit our website.

CHRISTOPHER THORNTON - COUNTY EDITOR
HERBERT EIDEN - ASSISTANT EDITOR
GEOFFREY HARE - CHAIR OF TRUST

www.victoriacountyhistory.ac.uk/counties/essex

GLOUCESTERSHIRE

Gloucestershire is a county of contrasts, from the high Cotswolds in the east, across the fertile Severn vale, and westward to the Forest of Dean. Its landscape variety is matched by a highly distinctive heritage. Its natural resources were the foundation for extensive monastic ownership, its traces still apparent today. Gloucestershire can boast distinctive rural and extractive industries, a wealth of gentry houses and royal connections, and strong sporting traditions — not least Robert Dover's 400-year-old Olympick Games. The county's horizons widened in the 20th century, building on craft traditions to lead in aviation, and then, in the form of GCHQ, to lead again in another new field.

The ten VCH volumes already issued capture much of this rich Gloucestershire variety, documenting and explaining change. The latest volumes show especially what a wealth of history can be brought to light through modern scholarship. With nearly half the county now written up in big red books, yet with a big gap in South Gloucestershire, and bare patches elsewhere, there is rising demand for the job to be finished. The interest in local history has never been stronger and everyone wants 'their' parish to be next!

Since the withdrawal of public funding in 2010, the VCH locally has been supported by the Gloucestershire County History Trust. Work had halted with the latest volume, covering a dozen Severn-side parishes, only part-finished, and the trust's first priority has been to secure its completion. A freelance editor has now been contracted to do this by late 2013. The resumed research and writing has been funded by an early wave

Market Day in Chipping Campden, taken by local photographer Jesse Taylor, c.1910. The VCH is above all else a history of a county's people and how they have exploited our landscape (for better or worse), and shaped our villages and towns. Like other Cotswold towns, Chipping Campden was originally built on wealth from wool — perhaps some pigs too — but latterly also became a centre for arts and crafts, for horticultural research, and most recently tourism and recreation. The full story of Campden and its surrounding area is to be explored in the next stage of VCH Gloucestershire (image courtesy of CADHAS).

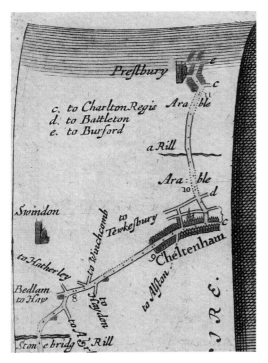

A section from John Ogilby's Britannia Atlas of 1675. *Ogilby broke new ground with the accuracy of his mapping, though any VCH coverage of Cheltenham will not make his mistake in placing the parish church north of the High Street, as here (image courtesy of Gloucestershire Archives).*

of donations from across the county, including a sponsored walk which raised over £3,000.

This though is only the first step, and the trust is working now to ensure an orderly continuation of work beyond 2013, to tackle remaining gaps in a pragmatic way. The business plan envisages around 18 further volumes (and online versions) to complete the county, the rate of progress being crucially dependent on the amount of funding. Indicative costings have been established for researching and writing up all the unfinished parishes, based on their relative size (acres and population) and complexity (rural, town, industrial and so on). Figures start at around £12,000 for a small parish, which can initially seem daunting, but once digested is actually something that a local community fundraising initiative can be built around: it forms a comprehensible target, to be coupled with volunteer effort, philanthropy, related local projects and funding bids as appropriate.

This approach has much to commend it — new parish histories once completed can be published online straightaway, with hard-copy (Big Red Book or another format) coming later. We can start work concurrently in different parts of the county, thus helping to satisfy more of the 'us next' parishes, which often have a strong base of active local history volunteers who, under professional guidance, can be drafted in for vital spade-work.

In an environment where community groups and charities are increasingly attuned to running projects and making connections, 'doing local history' can actually support, and be integrated with, other initiatives: a bid for local regeneration is greatly strengthened by a well-documented statement of the area's heritage. Parish-based localism is also more likely to identify and tap into serious local philanthropy. In Gloucestershire, we are under no illusions about being able to carry on producing the VCH solely through individual subscriptions, vital as they have been to get us on the road again, and welcome as they continue to be. For every parish tackled from now on, a significant personal donation will be required and such generosity will of course be acknowledged in the final publication, in the great VCH tradition.

Sir Nicholas Mander - Chair of Trust, James Hodsdon - Honorary Treasurer
John Chandler - Consultant Editor

www.victoriacountyhistory.ac.uk/counties/gloucestershire

HAMPSHIRE

The first of all VCH counties to be published, in 1900, was *Hampshire* I. Few counties needed the Victoria County History as much as Hampshire. Earlier county histories were abortive and Hampshire was slow to establish its county society and journal (Hampshire Field Club, 1885) or record series (Hampshire Record Society, 1892). It was the VCH that established the hundred and parish framework and surveyed the manors, parish churches and charities that underpinned all subsequent histories. Now online and free of charge (www.british-history.ac.uk), VCH Hampshire is a worldwide resource that attracts thousands of hits each year. It is an outsider's view, based on sources in London printed and unprinted. Like other early county sets, it made little use of local expertise and local resources, sometimes second to none: the bishop of Winchester's pipe rolls, Winchester College, and the archives of Oxford colleges. Since 1914 Hampshire has developed: Bournemouth, Portsmouth and Southampton as conurbations, Andover and Basingstoke as new towns; its archives have become accessible and have been published by three record series; Pevsner's *Buildings of England Hampshire* is reaching a second edition; and much more has been written by postgraduates at the county's universities and by a myriad of local societies.

Hampshire VCH suffered the limitations of prototypes completed before the First World War. There were simple errors, for example the mislocation of some places, and history itself has moved on. VCH volumes now routinely include economic and social history, all religious denominations, and religious and secular buildings.

The need to correct, update, and expand the Hampshire VCH has long been recognised. The New VCH Hampshire was launched in 2007 by four key players — Hampshire Archives Trust, Hampshire County Council, Hampshire Field Club and Archaeological Society, and the University of Winchester — which form the New VCH Hampshire Partnership. The aim is to rewrite Hampshire by place in about 13 volumes over the next half century. Two red books are underway: a parish volume on the chalk downlands to the east and south of Basingstoke and a history of Basingstoke itself. Basingstoke was selected because it has been transformed since 1914 due to London overspill. The parish volume centres on Basing House of Civil War fame, and Steventon, birthplace of Jane Austen. The target is one volume in five years and the other in another five.

Since new red books lie in the future, it is fortunate that modern technology permits interim publications that can reach a much larger audience much more quickly than in the past. The new article for Mapledurwell is already published online.

A mosaic of parishes or sections are posted ahead of the volumes that bring the whole together. Volunteers can witness at once their contributions to a prestigious national enterprise. Volunteers compete to make short postings on such items as the Massagainian riots of 1881–5 in Basingstoke or Jane Austen in Steventon on the VCH Explore site (explore.englandspastforeveryone.org.uk).

Research is undertaken by about 30 volunteers, many from Basingstoke Archaeological and Historical Society, who bring invaluable local knowledge to the project. They are trained and led by a professional coordinator, Dr Jean Morrin. A fortnightly meeting in Basingstoke digests copies of wills and inventories 1500–1700 towards the economic, social and religious life chapters of parish histories and imparts the palaeographical skills needed for independent work at record offices. Maps, trade directories, parliamentary papers online and the census are also studied. Some volunteers also meet alternate weeks with the coordinator at Hampshire Record Office, which provides tutorial classes on particular records. Further support and some writing up is undertaken by academics and other experts. Especially rewarding has been the development of mutual support, particularly through familiarisation walks of parishes that terminate with a pub lunch! Several topics and parishes are researched simultaneously, mainly on the 19th and 20th centuries. Some volunteers specialise on the Basingstoke economy, others on the parishes. Mapledurwell is finished, Steventon and Up Nately fairly advanced, and work progresses on Ellisfield, Herriard, Nately Scures, Newnham, North Waltham, Old Basing, Upton Grey and Western Patrick.

The project connects communities, disseminates historical skills and raises the standard of other local history. Whilst there are no salaries to pay, recurrent costs are room hire, photocopying and travel of volunteers and the coordinator that up to now have been generously defrayed by charities (Marc Fitch Fund, Charlotte Bonham-Carter and Bulldog Trusts) and by support in kind. To continue the project needs expert assistance, particularly on earlier history, more volunteers, and donations and grants of about £5,000 a year.

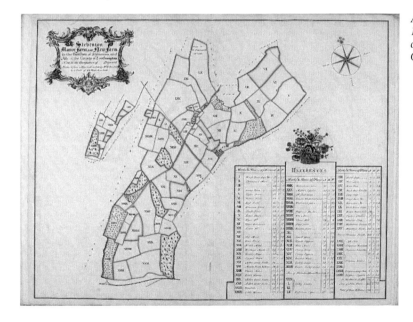

A map of Steventon from 1741 (image courtesy of Hampshire Record Office).

JEAN MORRIN - TEAM LEADER

www.victoriacountyhistory.ac.uk/counties/hampshire

HEREFORDSHIRE

Herefordshire is a border county; its western parishes lay within the Welsh Marches in the Middle Ages, and the ruins of several medieval border castles survive, notably at Goodrich, Longtown, Wigmore and Clifford. The cathedral city of Hereford is the only large town in the county, but there are five small market towns: Leominster, Ledbury, Bromyard, Ross and Kington. The county is famous for its timber-framed buildings, several villages in the north-west of the county having a large number of surviving early examples. The rich soil of the central plain of Herefordshire has sustained a prosperous agricultural community for much of its history, producing at different times grain, cider apples, hops, and soft fruits; livestock grazed on rich water meadows include brown and white Herefordshire cattle. The Malvern Hills on the eastern boundary and the Black Mountains on the west historically provided rough grazing but are now increasingly used for recreation.

Although numerous local antiquaries and historians collected material for a history of Herefordshire from the 17th century onwards, no such history has yet been completed. The incomplete one started by John Duncumb in 1804 and discontinued after 1913 is, as its name implies, more a collection of transcripts and commentary than a coherent history. The VCH published one volume on Herefordshire, covering antiquities and Domesday Book, in 1908; work on a second volume was discontinued in 1909 when the central VCH was in difficulties. Moves to revive the Herefordshire VCH started in the early 1990s and the Trust for the Victoria County History of Herefordshire was set up in 1998. The Trust participated in the England's Past for Everyone project between 2005 and 2009, centred on Ledbury. Since 2009 it has been able to finance some continuing work on the Ledbury region and is also working to raise the profile of the VCH in Herefordshire, where many people do not know how valuable the VCH can be to local and family historians.

A good start has been made with the Ledbury volumes in the EPE series. Of course more than 250 parish histories, and the history of the city of Hereford, will need to be researched and written to complete the VCH project but individual parish histories are relatively affordable, taking a full-time researcher only about six months to write. We hope that by starting with such individual parish histories we can eventually produce red books, covering wider areas. The first Red Book has already been begun, building on our research into the market town Ledbury and extending it into the neighbouring parishes, including Eastnor and Bosbury, which will be mounted on our website as soon as they are written.

The EPE project has taught us the value, and also some of the limitations, of volunteers. The Ledbury work benefited enormously from the enthusiasm and dedication of 30–40 volunteers. With training provided by the team leader and a retired VCH editor acting as volunteer group leader, they were able to tackle sources ranging from a medieval rental to oral history. We may not have the resources to organise quite as many volunteers in future, but their work will continue to be vital to the project. We shall need a professional historian to write up the volunteers' work and to carry out research in some of the earlier and more difficult documents, and in archives outside

The ruins of Goodrich Castle dominate a bend in the river Wye. Beyond, the central Herefordshire plain spreads its fertile fields (image courtesy of Janet Cooper)

Herefordshire, as well as to oversee the project as a whole. We would also hope to be able to employ experts who could contribute, on contract or voluntarily, specialist knowledge to the parish and town histories. To this end the Trust is seeking support in cash or kind and doing its utmost to promote the VCH. It publishes a biannual newsletter containing details of its activities and short historical articles.

SYLVIA PINCHES - TEAM LEADER
JANET COOPER - CHAIRMAN OF TRUST

www.victoriacountyhistory.ac.uk/counties/herefordshire

KENT

When Kent was selected to form part of the Heritage Lottery Funded England's Past for Everyone project in 2005, volunteer research into new paperback histories on the county ended a long break in VCH activity there. Initial work had stopped in 1932, with three volumes of the VCH Kent series completed in a county which, as the editor William Page admitted in volume I, had been 'peculiarly attractive' to historians since the sixteenth century. The VCH volumes covered standard general topics such as natural history, ancient earthworks, ecclesiastical history, religious houses and Kent's Domesday. A long section on Romano-British remains was compiled by a large team which included two famous professors of archaeology, Haverfield and Wheeler.

Until 2005 no progress had been made on Kent's parishes. Since then two EPE paperbacks have covered several parishes around the river Medway. They present a very different picture of the county from the conventional one of the 'Garden of England', with its abundance of orchards, hop gardens and largely agricultural landscape. Indeed, in the first book – *The Medway Valley: A Kent Landscape Transformed* – Dr Andrew Hann, using the work of a large team of volunteers, charts how the lower Medway valley changed from a quiet agrarian region into an Industrial centre of cement, brick and paper manufacture. One chapter – written by John Newman, author of the Kent Pevsner guides – discusses what it was like to live in three of the villages in the 18th and 19th centuries and how they evolved physically into what we see today.

Aylesford, photographed from the 14th-century stone bridge that crosses the Medway.

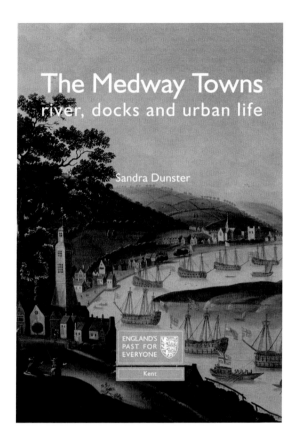

The second history (forthcoming 2013) has been researched and written by Dr Sandra Dunster, who also contributed to the Medway Valley story. It explores *The Medway Towns: river, docks and urban life*, describing the development of the communities who lived and worked in the cathedral city of Rochester and the towns of Chatham, Strood and Gillingham, and how those towns merged physically but developed distinct characteristics.. The most dramatic changes were caused by the growth of the Royal Naval Dockyards at Chatham, home to the English fleet from the 16th to the 18th century, which became the largest industrial complex in the south of England.

At least two more projects are to be carried out with the help of volunteers, resulting in a paperback history of Sevenoaks, a town transformed by its position on the fringe of London, another on the ancient port of Faversham. There may be a third paperback, on parishes associated with the stretch of the coast most famous for the Cinque Ports. With financial support as well as the local enthusiasm for research already shown, more projects can continue to cover the county of Kent.

LEICESTERSHIRE

Leicestershire is a diverse and dynamic county, celebrated for its deserted villages, mines and quarries, knitting and hosiery, and ethnic diversity. It has a history of innovations: Robert Bakewell experimented with selective breeding on its pastures; Robert Stephenson built an early railway; and Thomas Cook pioneered mass tourism.

It also has a proud historical tradition, and Leicestershire's VCH should have been completed long ago. In the early days, before the First World War, Leicestershire had an active county society, and a tradition of writing parish histories represented by Burton (1622) and Nichols (1795–1815), but only one VCH volume appeared. By the late 1940s the University of Leicester was a leader in the academic study of local history, and the subject's chief proponent, W.G. Hoskins, revived the Leicestershire VCH and raised funds, mainly from the city and county councils. He commissioned two more general volumes, with distinguished authors such as J.H. Plumb, Rodney Hilton and Joan Thirsk. With the approval of VCH Central Office, Hoskins then introduced two innovations: Volume IV was devoted to the history of Leicester (www.british-history.ac.uk/source.aspx?pubid=527), and was the first VCH volume to cover a single town or city, while volume V, covering south-east Leicestershire (www.british-history.ac.uk/source.aspx?pubid=98), included a section on the economic history of each parish, a plan which

A field trip in April 2011 gave Leicestershire volunteers an opportunity to consider how the rich evidence preserved within the fabric and fittings of our parish churches can provide clues to changes in village population, wealth, religious beliefs and also the secular needs of the parish. The volunteers are pictured outside Mowsley, which retains many medieval features, including three 13th-century piscinae and a stone mensa.

was subsequently adopted nationally. By 1964, the money was exhausted and publication ceased.

A third surge of activity is now addressing the 300 town and village histories which remain to be researched and written. A County Trust was formed in 2008–9, with a committee including the County Archivist, the secretary of the Archaeological Society, academics from the University of Leicester and others with an enthusiasm for the county's history. A lawyer from one of Leicester's leading firms assisted with registration as a charitable company. Various events have been organised, including launches at Quenby Hall, a stately home and County Hall. They attracted a large number of guests, but the most successful in terms of fundraising (and in attracting goodwill) was a public lecture by Michael Wood, a patron, who based his very successful *Story of England* TV series on the Leicestershire village of Kibworth. The Trust has a successful Friends scheme, although the main sources of funds have been the County Council, the University of Leicester and local charitable trusts.

The Trust is now pursuing a two-pronged approach to take the VCH forward. We have an active and enthusiastic group of 40 volunteers, researching the history of county parishes under the guidance of a coordinator, a process that began with a successful event at the local BBC headquarters. The funds we have raised enable us to provide workshops to help our volunteers use and interpret a wide range of documents and occasional field trips, to provide training in the interpretation of non-documentary sources. The volunteers have also spent an introductory day at the National Archives (TNA) at Kew. As part of our parish history research, transcripts of probate inventories are being added to the VCH website, for the benefit of other local and family historians.

The second strategy has been to apply to the HLF for money to embark on a study of Charnwood in north Leicestershire. Most of rural Leicestershire is quite flat, agricultural and dominated by nucleated villages. Charnwood has jagged peaks, extensive heaths, woodland, industry and scattered settlements. Our initial application, under the title *Charnwood Roots*, was successful and the project development is now being funded by the HLF. If awarded, the grant will make possible a community-based history project involving 400 volunteers over four years. With support from historians, volunteers will discover how interactions between people and landscape over many centuries have shaped the Charnwood of today. Archival research will form the core of the project but our research activities will extend to oral history, archaeological digs and building and landscape surveys. Four themes will be researched: working lives, crime and conflict, building communities and landscapes of leisure. The project will produce parish histories for a Red Book but we will also reach new audiences through a travelling exhibition, web resources, educational packs and a heritage festival, open to all, to celebrate this ever-changing area of Leicestershire.

PAMELA FISHER - VOLUNTEER CO-ORDINATOR
JULIE DEEMING - PROJECT DEVELOPMENT OFFICER
SQUIRE DE LISLE - CHAIR OF TRUST

www.victoriacountyhistory.ac.uk/counties/leicestershire

MIDDLESEX

For those who value the survival of the identity of ancient counties, VCH Middlesex is a treasure. While the VCH volumes provide detailed coverage of Greater London, they all belong to the VCH sets devoted to Middlesex, Essex and Surrey. The reason for such an arrangement dates back to the origins of the VCH in 1899. Although the London County Council was established ten years before the VCH, the founders of the History chose to publish it all in sets devoted to the ancient counties. Consequently, they planned to tackle Middlesex and Surrey hundred by hundred, parish by parish including the parishes already within London's boundaries (the Essex parishes were embraced by later boundary changes). The original plan was soon changed and it was decided to produce three volumes on London (defined as London within the Bars, Southwark borough, and Westminster ancient parish), but only a single volume (*London* I (1909) on archaeology and religious houses) ever appeared. A fuller treatment of Southwark awaits the revision of *VCH Surrey* IV (1912), but a history of the City of Westminster is now being written as part of *VCH Middlesex*.

Although the London project had foundered, work on Middlesex went ahead separately, one volume (II, containing general articles and parish histories) being published in 1911 before all work on the VCH stopped in 1915. It was not until 1955 that *VCH Middlesex* was revived. Then, with the support of the county council and local boroughs, it began by publishing on the areas of Middlesex outside the LCC boundary, continuing with that plan after 1965 when Middlesex's administrative independence was abolished and the London Boroughs took over support. In traditional VCH fashion work progressed hundred by hundred, west to east through Outer Middlesex from Spelthorne, Elthorne, Gore and Edmonton hundreds (volumes II to V) and covering parishes from Staines to South Mimms to Ealing and Hornsey in the fringes of Ossulstone hundred (volumes VI to VII). Then work began on London's core, the former LCC part of Ossulstone hundred, with parishes in the London Boroughs of Islington, Camden, Westminster, Hackney, Tower Hamlets, and Kensington & Chelsea (volumes VIII to XIII). This magnificent effort left only the London Borough of Hammersmith & Fulham and the City of Westminster completely untouched by 2004.

VCH Middlesex, more than any other VCH project, has a particular character. One challenge has been the vast amount of documentary evidence available, both locally and in the London Metropolitan Archive and TNA, as well as thousands of complementary published books and articles, the result of long and intense interest in London and its surroundings. Secondly, the sheer scale of physical development is daunting; in many areas the VCH has left the accounts in *The Survey of London*, founded five years before the VCH, stand as the main source on that subject. But there could hardly be a more interesting project, with places ranging from the riverside village of Isleworth (III) to the sophisticated urbanity of The Strand (XIII), and a history embracing changes as dramatic as the transformation of the hamlet of Bethnal Green (XI) into the archetypal East End slum and the obliteration by the creation of London airport of all but one magnificent medieval barn, now in the care of English Heritage (www.english-heritage.org.uk/daysout/properties/harmondsworth-barn), to show the investment Winchester College made in its manor of Harmondsworth (IV).

A history of the City of Westminster presents distinct but fascinating challenges. Westminster not only has an incomparable place in national affairs but also has a rich and

The design of James Gibbs's 18th-century church for Westminster's ancient parish of St Martin-in-the-Fields has been become one of the most imitated in the western world. VCH Middlesex XIII: The City of Westminster, Landownership and Religious History tells the story not only of that church and its predecessors, built on the site of a Romano-British cemetery, but also of the religious life of the parish.

much less well-known local history. With one volume (XIII, *Landownership and Religious History)* published in 2010, research for volume XIV is now uncovering Westminster's social history, as well as its complex layers of local government with an enduring pattern of overlapping authorities. The project is supported by a thriving Westminster History Club, and by donations to the County History Trust. Our aim during the Jubilee year is to begin several projects: researching a history of St Clement Danes parish, displaying many discoveries about Westminster's charities, educational establishments and places of entertainment on VCH Explore, and raising £60,000 to finish the whole of volume XIV as a celebration of 60 years' work on the revived Middlesex VCH.

To find out more about Middlesex VCH, the Westminster History Club, and how to contribute to the history of Westminster by donating time, money or expertise, please visit our website.

PATRICIA CROOT - CONSULTANT EDITOR
ELIZABETH WILLIAMSON - PROJECT CO-ORDINATOR

www.victoriacountyhistory.ac.uk/counties/middlesex

NORTHAMPTONSHIRE

Northamptonshire developed in the 10th century as the territory belonging to the former Viking military and administrative centre of Northampton following its reconquest by the Anglo-Saxon king Edward in 918. Its historic boundaries extended from the fens around Peterborough in the north-east to the fertile hilly region between Daventry and Brackley in the south-west. The county's dominant natural feature is the river Nene, which flows north-eastwards through Northampton and Peterborough before emptying into the Wash. To its north and south wooded landscapes formed part of the royal forests of Rockingham, Salcey, and Whittlewood, while to its west lay the watershed between the Nene and Welland.

Northamptonshire is popularly known as a county of 'spires and squires'. Churches adorned with stone steeples proliferated in the later Middle Ages, but only in those areas close to freestone quarries or within easy reach of water transport. The limestones dug at Barnack, Stanion, Weldon and other quarries between Stamford and Corby were used by the county's squires for the country houses built from the 16th century. Impressive examples include the Spencers' house at Althorp, Kirby Hall, Lamport Hall and Thomas Tresham's unfinished Lyveden New Bield. Less prestigious building stones were more widely available, including the rich brown sandstones around Northampton, and darker ironstones, from which the village of Rockingham was largely built.

Ironstone dug from prehistoric times provided the basis of the county's important iron industry, which was revived in the 19th and 20th centuries, notably at the new steel-making town of Corby. The county's modern industrial heritage was explored in a pioneering VCH volume. Topographical volumes have covered the eastern side of the county along the Nene valley, including Northampton and Peterborough, and the rural area abutting Milton Keynes.

The VCH was revived in Northamptonshire in 1995 (after almost 60 years) when the Northamptonshire Victoria County History Trust was set up under the chairmanship of Lord Naseby. Generous support funded the employment of full-time county staff from 1996 to 2009, resulting in two red books and a paperback. In 2010, with Lord Boswell as Chairman, a new strategy was adopted: part-time consultants were appointed to write the history of Corby and Great Oakley. This means that work on the county's VCH can continue without large-scale fundraising, and it is expected the next volume will be written in a similar way, with significant contributions from local volunteers.

Volume VIII will cover Towcester hundred. Lactodorum was a military staging post on Watling Street, the Roman road from London to Chester; Towcester grew up on its site (the name means Roman camp on the river Tove) and in the Middle Ages boasted a castle, a fine church and a market. It stood at the head of the hundred which included the villages of Abthorpe, Cold Higham, Gayton, Pattishall and Tiffield. The addition of Towcester would bring the VCH's coverage in Northamptonshire to 12 of the county's 20 hundreds and would represent a significant step towards its completion.

LORD BOSWELL OF AYNHO - CHAIR OF TRUST

MATTHEW BRISTOW - CO-ORDINATOR
www.victoriacountyhistory.ac.uk/counties/northamptonshire

NOTTINGHAMSHIRE

The two general volumes for Nottinghamshire were published in 1906 and 1910. The first includes an edition of the Domesday text for the county by a young F.M. Stenton, whose home was at Southwell in south-east Nottinghamshire. Had Stenton remained involved with VCH and kept up his interest in the county, work might have continued in Nottinghamshire after the First World War and publication of the two topographical volumes promised on the title-page of the first in the series might have been achieved.

In the event, there seems to have been no thought of restarting work until 2009, when the county council, through Nottinghamshire Archives, made funds available to enable the part-time County Editor for Derbyshire, then a research fellow in the School of History at Nottingham University, to extend his work across the Erewash. From the outset, it was clear that progress in Nottinghamshire, even more than in Derbyshire, would depend on support from local historians in the county prepared to tackle parishes in which they had an existing interest and, if possible, others. Because of a strong tradition of good quality local history in Nottinghamshire, which owes much to the continuing education work of the University over a long period, support of this sort was quickly forthcoming. Following a series of exploratory meetings to explain the project, a group of experienced local historians have come together to meet at Nottinghamshire Archives once a fortnight to collect material for the history of particular parishes, led by the County Editor and helped by the preparation for the county of a 'Handbook' containing practical advice on how to write a VCH parish history. Although, after the initial two years of funding, the county council was unable to provide any further direct financial support for VCH, Nottinghamshire Archives have continued to make accommodation available for the project.

Good progress has been made over the last three years to re-establish VCH in Nottinghamshire. Work is underway on about a dozen parishes, although more activity in the north of the county would be welcome. Draft text is beginning to be mounted on the Nottinghamshire section of the website and a group of contiguous parishes has been identified that could make up a hardback volume. If the present level of support can be sustained, it should be possible to continue and perhaps accelerate progress. On the other hand, there is at present no fundraising body for VCH in Nottinghamshire. Essentially the work rests on the ability and willingness of the University to support a part-time County Editor's post and that of the volunteers to do the research. It would be a great pity to lose the momentum that has been built up since 2009 and perhaps the next step is to give VCH a firmer institutional identity. But even without this, it has proved possible for VCH to reclaim another county in the East Midlands, alongside Derbyshire and Leicestershire, from those where work has been in abeyance for a long time.

PHILIP RIDEN - COUNTY EDITOR

www.victoriacountyhistory.ac.uk/counties/nottinghamshire

OXFORDSHIRE

Oxfordshire is currently one of the more advanced VCH counties, with completion of the project a realistic target and an energetic fundraising Trust engaged with local partners to that end. The obstacles, chiefly financial, remain as daunting as ever; but with a spate of recent publications and a host of new initiatives in development, these are exciting if difficult times for a county project originally started in 1907.

Probably most famous for its university and 20th-century car industry, Oxfordshire remains a richly diverse and still largely agricultural county, stretching from the wooded and thinly settled Chilterns to the edge of the Cotswolds and, further north, to the ironstone redlands of 'Banburyshire'. VCH coverage is broadly spread, despite the geographical gaps which the Trust is determined to fill. Recent or imminent publications have dealt with parts of central and west Oxfordshire and the Chilterns and another Chiltern volume is scheduled for completion in 2015–16. Oxford itself has two volumes covering the city and university and, of the county's market towns, only Chipping Norton remains untouched.

Work on the county began early, with general volumes in 1907 and 1939. There followed a hiatus until a County Committee was set up in 1949, championed by prominent Oxford historians as well as local worthies. The first 'topographical' volume appeared in 1957 and in 1965 Oxfordshire County Council, in the spirit of the times, took on primary responsibility. The council (with Oxford University's History Faculty)

Volunteers engaged in archaeological test-pitting at Ewelme on the edge of the Chilterns, one of the places currently being worked on by the Oxfordshire VCH. Archival research remains central to the VCH approach, but landscape and buildings are just as important. In the Ewelme area help from archaeological professionals and the South Oxfordshire Archaeological Group has allowed the VCH to promote small-scale excavations which are elucidating early settlement in this important part of the county, closely linked with London by river and road (photo © Dave Oliver, SOAG).

remains part of a three-way local partnership but, as in many VCH counties, the chief partner now is an independent VCH Trust, which was set up in 1997 and in 2011 became the principal funder. Run on a voluntary basis by a committed group of trustees from varied professional backgrounds, the Oxfordshire Trust has consistently raised over £50,000 a year towards the project's completion, driven by a passionate belief in its value and its importance to the county. The partnership currently supports three research staff including a County Editor. In Jubilee year, the vigorous support of successive Lord Lieutenants and several Deputy Lieutenants is worth mentioning.

Like the VCH as a whole, the Oxfordshire project has changed markedly over the years, while still recognisably remaining itself. In retrospect it was fortunate to be delayed — effectively until the 1950s–60s, a period when the VCH was emancipating itself from its antiquarian beginnings and expanding the range of topics covered. For their time many of the early Oxfordshire parish histories remain exemplary in their treatment of settlement, vernacular buildings and religious and social history, and since the 1970s the impact of new approaches has become ever more evident. This has been demonstrated in recent years by partnerships with such bodies as the Oxfordshire Buildings Record (OBR) and South Oxfordshire Archaeological Group (SOAG), whose members have contributed as volunteers to particular projects. The OBR played a pivotal role in EPE work on Burford, while SOAG has facilitated recent excavations, garden test-pitting and geophysical surveys in the Chilterns. All are symptomatic of the ways in which the Oxfordshire VCH is branching out into new and exciting areas and engaging with local communities.

Alongside these initiatives the VCH's intensive investigation of documentary sources continues. Partly because of the University of Oxford's presence the county is richly documented, with college archives such as those of Magdalen, Christ Church and St John's (all relevant to current research) retaining wide-ranging material dating in some instances from the 13th century. Other material resides in the county archives and much further afield. Here, too, expert volunteer groups are making a contribution, amongst them an Oxfordshire Probate Group originally set up for England's Past for Everyone, which is now turning its attention to the Chilterns.

VCH coverage of Oxfordshire as a whole is now more than two-thirds complete, with most of its 16 volumes available online and new volumes scheduled for Jubilee Year and 2015–16. Final completion is dependent on continued partnerships and above all on continued fundraising by the VCH Oxfordshire Trust. With adequate funding completion could be achieved in 15 to 20 years: not all that long for a project of such longevity and proven usefulness.

SIMON TOWNLEY - COUNTY EDITOR
KATE TILLER - CHAIR OF TRUST

www.victoriacountyhistory.ac.uk/counties/oxfordshire

SHROPSHIRE

A single general volume was produced for the VCH Shropshire set in 1908, which covered the standard topics of natural history, early man, Shropshire's entry in Domesday, ancient earthworks and industries. No further work was possible in Shropshire until 1961, when a Records Committee of the County Council was appointed and resumed work on the Shropshire series. Between 1961 and 1998, six further volumes were produced, two of which, under the editorship of George Baugh, were general volumes detailing Administrative History and Agriculture respectively. Volume IV on Shropshire's agriculture (1989) is one of the most widely cited VCH volumes, and serves as a model for modern general volumes.

After the publication of volume X in 1998, attention turned to the county town of Shrewsbury, which boasts a largely unaltered medieval street plan, over 600 listed buildings including some of the finest timber-framed buildings in England as well as Ditherington flax mill (the first iron-framed building in the world), a Norman castle, Shrewsbury abbey and the remains of the medieval town walls. County Editor George Baugh continued to work on this volume, following his retirement and the closure of the VCH Shropshire office in 2003, until 2007 when the VCH successfully applied for a grant from the Marc Fitch Fund to complete the Shrewsbury volume on a consultancy basis. The final publication will be a two-part urban volume, similar in content and character to the VCH Chester volumes published in 2003–05.

The first of the two parts is scheduled for publication in 2013. It will recount the history of the town from the early medieval period until the twenty-first century in a series of chapters written by experts. They include the archaeologist Dr Nigel Baker

A HISTORY OF SHROPSHIRE

may be found quite as often in hedges or even in bushes on hillsides at a considerable elevation. From its habit of singing at night it is sometimes mistaken for the nightingale, though the song is different, but the bird is a great mimic.

27. Grasshopper-Warbler. *Locustella nævia* (Boddaert)

A summer visitor thinly scattered throughout the county but nowhere numerous. Its curious trilling note may generally be heard about the end of April, but the bird itself is seldom seen owing to its shy skulking habits. It returns year after year to the same place, and there is a certain spot near Ironbridge where Mr. F. Rawdon Smith has heard it with unfailing regularity for more than twenty years. It seems generally to prefer damp situations, but is also found on rough ground along the sides of low hills.

28. Hedge - Sparrow. *Accentor modularis* (Linn.)

Resident and abundant everywhere. Its

31. Long-tailed Tit. *Acredula rosea* (Blyth)
Locally, Canbottlin, Canbottle, Mumruffin.

This is another charming little bird. Its lovely egg-shaped nest, so compactly woven and ornamented with lichens, etc., is more often found in the midst of a clump of rose brambles than elsewhere, though frequently placed in a gorse bush. It is built early in the year, and I have found eggs in it towards the end of March. Both parents may often be found in the nest at the same time. When sitting the long tail of the bird projects from the aperture of the nest and is turned forwards over its head. In autumn this tit goes about in family parties, flitting in long procession from tree to tree as it progresses through the woodland glades with incessant iteration of its call-note. In winter it associates also with other tits, goldcrests and tree-creepers. Perhaps no British bird has such a large and curious list of local names as the long-tailed tit. I have given the three that are commonly used in Shropshire, where the species is numerous.

An extract from Shropshire I *highlights the type of natural history-related material which was found in early volumes such as these.*

An 18th-century oil painting by John Webber depicting Abbey Mill, Shrewsbury (image: Shrewsbury Museums Service, public domain via Wikimedia Commons).

and Professor Richard Holt on Shrewsbury before 1200; Alan Thacker, Robert and the late Dorothy Cromarty on the town between 1200 and 1350, when Shrewsbury was of national importance; W.A. Champion on developments between 1350 and 1780 when the town within the walls achieved its current physical shape and character; and Barrie Trinder on modern Shrewsbury, its industrial development and suburban spread. Many of the themes touched on in the first publication will receive much fuller treatment in the second part. Particularly valuable will be well-illustrated sections on individual religious congregations and their buildings, institutions and their continuity, and topics particular to Shrewsbury such as the common lands, its county institutions, the town walls and castle, and the liberties and municipal boundaries.

No further work is planned for Shropshire, though with its rich industrial history there is great scope for a further general volume or for the continuation of the topographical coverage of the county if funding can be sourced.

SOMERSET

Somerset is a county which has always generated a strong sense of attachment and pride in its history. Many antiquarians have attempted a history of the county but only the Revd John Collinson succeeded in publishing a complete history by parish, although his entries are fairly brief and concerned mainly with the manors and churches. The idea of a Victoria County History was therefore greeted with enthusiasm in 1900. Despite many problems the first Somerset volumes of the History were published in 1906 and 1912 and were general volumes. Work on the History was revived in 1967 as a co-operative venture between London University and Somerset County Council. Volume III, the first topographical volume covering the Ilchester, Langport and Somerset areas, was published in 1974. Since then seven more volumes have been published, most recently a volume covering the Castle Cary area and a paperback history of Southern Exmoor.

A volume on the Queen Camel and Cadbury areas is being prepared for publication and research is underway on a volume covering Minehead and Dunster. Completed drafts of sections of unpublished volumes can be found on the Somerset website. We have plans to cover the Taunton area next before possibly moving on to the Frome and Ilminster areas. This would give some coverage of most parts of the modern county but with sufficient resources we aim to reach Bath, Weston-super-Mare and the outskirts of Bristol. Our websites have allowed us to reach out to a much wider global audience and attract people who might never see a red volume but who are fascinated by all aspects of history. Images and short notes on themes, people, places, buildings, industries, churches and other interesting subjects that have been discovered while working on the Victoria County History and related local history projects can be found on the Explore website (explore.englandspastforeveryone.org.uk). Somerset items range from prehistoric Banwell Bone Caves to elegant Barrington Court and from life on Anglo-Saxon Exmoor to modern horsehair weaving at Castle Cary.

Somerset is a maritime and moorland county with a diverse agricultural and industrial history. It is rich in local historic sources on the ground, in its museums and in its archives. Glastonbury Abbey and Tor, Wells Cathedral and Bishop's Palace, and Bath Abbey and Roman Baths are iconic historic sites but every Somerset town and village is full of historic buildings in daily use. The Somerset Building Research Group, often using our resources, is revealing that there are many more medieval and early modern buildings in Somerset than previously thought.

The fascination of Somerset people with their heritage is shown by the thousands who have flocked to the new Museum of Somerset housed in Taunton's medieval castle to see treasures such as the Low Ham pavement telling the story of Dido and Aeneas and the Frome Hoard of Roman coins.

The new Somerset Heritage Centre, officially opened by Prince Edward in December 2011, houses Somerset's vast archive collections dating back over thousand years. There are many rich family and estate archives, such as those of the Luttrells of Dunster, Trevelyans of Nettlecombe and Dickinsons of Kingweston, all of which form a major component of Victoria County History research.

As part of our general outreach we have regularly helped individuals and organisations with information, assisted them with their own research and provided talks and classes working closely with the Somerset Heritage and Library Service. In return we obtain valuable help with research. The Exmoor project in Somerset explored many areas surveying green lanes and abandoned farmsteads. Work with other volunteer groups has helped older children and adults to explore their own past and feel more rooted in their local community. We aim to continue to be major providers of accurate and accessible information to everyone on the many aspects of Somerset's history and to enthuse and inspire others to share our love of the past that shaped our present and without which our future would be bleak.

Nettlecombe Court and church sit in beautiful late 18th-century parkland in a fold of the Brendon Hills. The archives of the Trevelyan family from this house were invaluable in researching the history of the Quantock and Brendon area covered in volume V of the Somerset History. Their letters from the 15th to 19th centuries, published by the Somerset Record Society, are very revealing about the people who lived there (image courtesy of Mary Siraut).

MARY SIRAUT - COUNTY EDITOR

www.victoriacountyhistory.ac.uk/counties/somerset

STAFFORDSHIRE

Although of middling size, the historic county of Staffordshire is one of the most populous, containing the city of Stoke-on-Trent — unique in its more familiar name, the Potteries, derived from an industry that owed much to one of England's most original designers and entrepreneurs Josiah Wedgwood, and celebrated in the novels of Arnold Bennett. The historic county also includes the Black Country conurbation (now in the West Midlands), another highly distinctive region that was at the forefront of Britain's industrial development in the 19th century. But the county also contains the sparsely-populated Moorlands (centred on Leek with its strong 'northern' townscape of former silk mills) and Needwood Forest connected with Tutbury castle, a favourite resort in the 14th century of England's wealthiest aristocrat, the quasi-royal John of Gaunt. Also of special note is Lichfield, the birthplace of Dr Samuel Johnson but more importantly one of the earliest Christian centres in Anglo-Saxon England as the site of the cathedral of St Chad, the evangelist to the Mercians. Moreover, the county's Mercian heritage has recently come to national and international attention following the chance discovery of the Staffordshire Hoard only a few miles from Lichfield.

What links these places — Stoke, Walsall and West Bromwich, Leek, Tutbury and Lichfield — is that they have all been treated in volumes of the Staffordshire VCH, which has maintained a steady output since work was re-started in the county in the mid 1950s. Generously supported by Staffordshire County Council and Keele University, which

A panoramic view of Trentham Hall with its lake from the south in 1862, on oil, by Henry Lark Pratt (image © Newcastle-under-Lyme Museum and Art Gallery).

A detail from an Ordnance Survey map (1870s) highlighting the garden design found at Trentham Hall (image © Ordnance Survey).

both place the highest value on preserving and promoting the county's rich heritage, the Staffordshire volumes aim to provide detailed and accessible histories not only of the leading towns and cities, but also of lesser known villages and hamlets, which otherwise would never receive the scholarly attention they deserve.

Only a single volume had appeared before VCH Staffordshire was revived in the early 1950s. After its revival it was one of the first VCH counties to treat an urban area, when it worked on Stoke-on-Trent and Newcastle-under-Lyme, and a recent return to the north-west of the county has uncovered much new material about the area's long-standing industrial history, with hitherto unknown accounts of early coal mining and iron working. Volume XI soon to appear also treats Trentham Hall and its spectacular 19th-century formal gardens created for the dukes of Sutherland, then one of the country's richest families. Their vast archive was recently purchased by the county council and is one of several collections that helped the Staffordshire and Stoke-on-Trent joint archive service to gain Designated Status in 2011. The Staffordshire VCH volumes therefore greatly benefit from the county's rich documentary resources, not least in the William Salt Library in Stafford, with its exceptional collection of Anglo-Saxon charters.

Attention is now being directed towards Tamworth in the far south-east, as part of a plan to ensure that no area of the county has to wait too long for its own volume, and also to raise its profile as a royal centre in the Anglo-Saxon kingdom of Mercia. The completion of the entire set to cover the historic county can now be seen as an achievable goal — provided that support remains forthcoming. Certainly, many people who have been active in researching their own communities have also been generous in providing information for inclusion in a VCH volume, and volunteer groups based at the Staffordshire Record Office are now doing valuable work on the Tamworth area. The county has also benefited from having had only three principal authors (styled County Editors) since work was resumed: L. Margaret Midgley, Michael Greenslade and now Nigel Tringham. Indeed, the present County Editor reckons that he has written not far short of a million words for six volumes since he arrived in the county.

NIGEL TRINGHAM - COUNTY EDITOR

www.victoriacountyhistory.ac.uk/counties/staffordshire

SUSSEX

Sussex is one of the most varied of the English counties in geology and landscape. Its extended coastline (*c.* 80 miles long) has cliffs of both chalk and sandstone, reclaimed marshland at both its eastern and western extremities and also some of the country's best-known seaside resorts. Inland lie broad river valleys and fertile farmland, well settled in Roman times and earlier. Further inland still is the remote woodland of the Weald, whose inhospitable terrain caused rural and urban development to be longer delayed.

Much of the county has already been covered in volumes in the topographical series of VCH Sussex. The latest have included the histories of older urban centres like Arundel, Shoreham and Horsham, and more modern ones like Littlehampton and Worthing. Within areas of the county not yet surveyed, the medieval towns of Petworth and East Grinstead call out for similar treatment. Among seaside places, while an earlier history of Brighton is currently undergoing revision (for publication as a separate volume), a full account of the premier resort of Eastbourne is much to be desired as well.

To match the VCH's recent coverage of Arundel Castle, Petworth House, one of the great residences of England set in an Arcadian Capability Brown landscape, also deserves a comprehensive history. Here, as at Arundel too, an extensive archive is still preserved in situ; it would provide rich detail for both social and architectural history.

Map of Sussex c. 2000, showing Parham House (subject of an EPE paperback in 2009) in relation to the chief towns in the 16th and 17th centuries, where aristocratic and gentry families were engaged in building and rebuilding their great houses. The high ground closest to the coast is the South Downs, that further north the Sussex Weald.

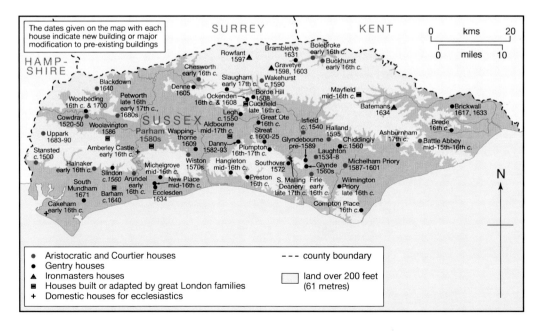

In landscape history one of Sussex's most intriguing features is the vast expanse of Ashdown Forest, once a royal domain, and still retaining aspects of a medieval wilderness despite proximity to the corridor of urbanisation between London and Brighton. A mine of documentation survives here, too, never as yet quarried by historians.

To finish the Sussex topographical volumes would take considerably less time and money than for many other counties. And Sussex has a special place in VCH history. William Page, the founding General Editor of the History (1902–34), long kept all its research notes in a storehouse in his garden at Middleton-on-Sea near Bognor Regis; while L.F. Salzman, an early contributor and the third General Editor (1934–49), lived in Lewes and was an important figure in the Sussex Archaeological Society.

That old-established body is part of a distinguished tradition in Sussex historiography that goes back to the voluminous collections of notes made by antiquaries like Sir William Burrell in the late 18th century; Burrell's notes and others too are preserved in the British Library for use by future historians. Completion of the Sussex VCH set would be a fitting way to honour the memory of such a long line of local enthusiasts.

TIM HUDSON - FORMER COUNTY EDITOR
SUE BERRY - BRIGHTON AND HOVE EDITOR

www.victoriacountyhistory.ac.uk/counties/sussex

BRIGHTON AND HOVE

In an attempt to persuade the Brighton parish vestry to build a spire for the 'New Church' which he designed, Charles Barry produced this fine print in the mid 1820s. The vestry decided that it could not afford this project (image © Sue Berry).

Part of the VCH's great effort to complete coverage of the whole of Susex is the research being done by Dr Sue Berry and her team of volunteers on Brighton & Hove. This complex new city, with a population in 2001 of almost half a million people, is the largest place to be tackled by the VCH since Birmingham in the 1960s. The aim is to produce a lasting work of reference, a sophisticated and readable urban biography and a story of English seaside culture to complement the recent VCH history of the north-east Essex resorts.

WILTSHIRE

Founded in 1947, the Victoria History of Wiltshire was the result of post-war innovation, a partnership between the IHR and local authorities. The collaboration was so successful that it became the model for work in other counties and helped to revive the VCH. It was the brainchild of David Murray John, clerk of Swindon Borough Council, and Ralph Pugh, the first editor of the Wiltshire series and a future General Editor; their Wiltshire VCH Committee was supported by Wiltshire County Council, Salisbury and Swindon borough councils, Wiltshire Archaeological and Natural History Society, the dioceses of Salisbury and Bristol and interested individuals. Local government reorganisation in 1974 brought support from the four district councils of Kennet, North Wiltshire, Salisbury and West Wiltshire. The two main funders today are the unitary Wiltshire Council, established in 2009, and since 2004, the University of the West of England, where Wiltshire VCH is based in the Regional History Centre. The project enjoys strong support from the county's local history community, working closely with Wiltshire Record Society, Wiltshire Local History Forum and Wiltshire Family History Society. The Wiltshire VCH Appeal Trust raises funds for exhibition and publicity materials, for a bursary for a UWE post graduate who contributes research, and for making Wiltshire volumes available online.

The population of Wiltshire, the largest inland county in southern England, is fragmented by Salisbury Plain at the centre. The landscapes around the Plain supported different forms of agriculture and industry according to their geology and natural resources. The well-known division between chalk and cheese gave rise to sheep and corn agriculture on the southern chalklands and dairying on the clay vales of the north. Wiltshire was industrialised early, producing cloth from the 13th century, also malt for brewing, mutton, bacon and cheese to feed England's growing 18th-century cities. The five towns of West Wiltshire — Bradford-on-Avon, Melksham, Trowbridge, Warminster and Westbury — became heavily industrialised in the 19th century. The building of the Great Western Railway caused Chippenham to grow, and saw the rise of the railway town of Swindon, which reinvented itself in the later 20th century by hosting new technology industries.

About three-quarters of the whole county has now been covered in 18 'big red books'. While volumes I–V tackle general themes, VI–XVIII are topographical volumes containing the histories of individual towns and villages. Volume XIX, on Longleat and the Deverill Valley, is in progress, and five more volumes are planned to complete the series. The research is widely available, with published volumes freely searchable on British History Online (www.british-history.ac.uk/place.aspx?gid=36&region=3), draft parish histories posted on the VCH Wiltshire website; and information incorporated in Wiltshire Council's Community History web pages. In addition, seven off-prints have been published on individual communities, in collaboration with local government and voluntary organisations, and two more — on Cricklade and Purton from volume XVIII — are being considered. Wiltshire was the first county to produce a paperback, researched with volunteer help, in the HLF-funded England's Past for Everyone series: *Codford: Wool and War in Wiltshire* (Phillimore, 2007). A companion volume on

Lamb Down, east of Codford, a chalk downland rich in prehistoric monuments and finds of flint and early metalwork. Many monuments are still visible on the ground or in aerial photographs (image courtesy of English Heritage: Mike Hesketh-Roberts).

Longleat is being written, and for Volume XIX volunteer researchers are transcribing Wiltshire wills previously digitised with HLF funding.

VCH Wiltshire staff work with experts in many heritage organisations, both professional and voluntary. The VCH Wiltshire team co-operate with staff of the Wiltshire and Swindon History Centre, (www.wshc.eu) to exploit its rich archives and local studies collections, many of which tell the stories of ordinary people. To ensure comprehensive coverage the VCH consults other collections, such as the archives at Longleat. They show how the Thynne family acquired lands which belonged to Glastonbury Abbey before its dissolution in 1539, and once formed part of the great pre-Conquest estate of Devrel with origins in the Iron Age culture of the Upper Wylye Valley.

VCH Wiltshire has produced an invaluable — and in some respects —pioneering body of knowledge about the county's heritage. The volumes, benefiting from advice from leading academics, were the first in the whole VCH to cover an expanded range of topics, for it was in VCH Wiltshire IV that well-known historians, including M.W. Beresford, W.G. Hoskins, F.M.L. Thompson and E.M. Carus Wilson, helped to develop the new themes of economic and social history. The tradition of academic excellence continues through the employment of two full-time professional historians, who receive valuable support from colleagues at UWE. Consequently Wiltshire's series of big red books has become the first point of reference for academics, local government officers, family and local historians, tourists and school children. The Wiltshire VCH Appeal Trust is energetically seeking support to ensure research continues until every parish has its own history.

VIRGINIA BAINBRIDGE - COUNTY EDITOR
ALEX CRAVEN - ASSISTANT COUNTY EDITOR
VICTORIA LANDELL-MILLS - CHAIR OF TRUST

www.victoriacountyhistory.ac.uk/counties/wiltshire

YORKSHIRE EAST RIDING

The East Riding has a landscape, economy and culture that distinguishes it from the rest of Yorkshire. It is part of lowland England with a landscape that belongs more to the south than the north. Outside the city of Hull, the resorts and fishing ports on the coast, and Beverley and the smaller market towns, the economy of the riding has been almost solely based on agriculture. No rural area of England of similar extent has been for so many centuries virtually devoid of extractive or manufacturing industries. The agriculture has been predominantly arable and until the 20th century much of the area was held by great estates and farmed by tenants. A surprising number of the landed families, some of whom have been resident from the Middle Ages, still own at least part of their former estates and live in their country houses, including Burton Agnes, Burton Constable and Sledmere.

The present landscape, although rich in prehistoric remains, is very much a creation of these landowners in the late 18th–early 19th centuries following the inclosure of the open arable fields and pastures. Then came the large hedged fields, the long straight roads with wide verges and the isolated farmsteads surrounded by plantations or shelter belts which characterise so much of the landscape, particularly of the Wolds. The new large farms were worked by young men who lived-in and were hired by the year, an employment system that lasted here up to the Second World War, far longer than in any other arable area. The mobility of this agricultural work force partly explains the lack of a strong folk culture, also eroded by the strength of Nonconformity. In 1851 the East Riding was the fourth most dissenting 'county' in England; only Cornwall had higher attendances at Methodist chapels. Almost every village had a Wesleyan and a Primitive Methodist chapel, as well as a parish church, of which the East Riding has some of the country's finest examples. There are splendid medieval churches such as St Patrick's, Patrington and the Minster and St. Mary's at Beverley, as well as many superb Victorian village churches by leading architects and craftsmen.

Much of this history has been recorded in the nine volumes so far completed, but the challenge now is to complete the task. More than two-thirds of the East Riding has been covered by the volumes already published, but a significant part of the Wolds and the Vale of York has yet to be done including the market towns of Pocklington, Market Weighton and Howden. Research is underway on the last and we are grateful for the ongoing support of the East Riding of Yorkshire Council, North Yorkshire County Council and the University of Hull, but if the work is to continue additional funds are needed urgently, together with the help of volunteer researchers.

The resources are excellent for the local historian with a wealth of archive sources, including the records of the major landed estates, available in three state-of-the-art repositories: the Treasure House at Beverley, Hull History Centre and the Borthwick Institute for Archives at the University of York.

DAVID NEAVE - CONSULTANT EDITOR
SUSAN NEAVE - CONSULTANT EDITOR

www.victoriacountyhistory.ac.uk/counties/yorkshire-east-riding

Middleton on the Wolds. The landscape, agriculture and buildings of this typical village on the Yorkshire Wolds were transformed after the inclosing of the open fields in 1805. Seven new farms were built at a distance from the settlement and the old village farmhouses and cottages, formerly of chalk, mud and thatch, were rebuilt in brick and pantile. The population increased from 286 in 1801 to 701 in 1861 (image courtesy of David & Susan Neave).

Wressle Castle on the river Derwent to the north of Howden, built c. 1380, was one of the favourite residences of the Percys, earls of Northumberland in the 15th- and early-16th century. The castle was reduced to its present size during the Civil Wars to prevent it from getting into the hands of the Royalists and it was gutted by fire in 1796. The Percys, major landowners in the East Riding, also spent time at their manor house at Leconfield, north of Beverley (image courtesy of David & Susan Neave).

Professor Christopher Elrington editing VCH texts in the General Editor's office in the IHR. A portrait of his predecessor, R.B. Pugh, hangs on the wall and rows of red books and boxes of VCH archives line the shelves.

BIOGRAPHIES OF NOTABLE CONTRIBUTORS

Since its inception the VCH has been created by a combination of professional scholars writing to contract, staff members employed through the central office and, since 1945, by County Editors based locally. Throughout the 20th century the General Editor was responsible for commissioning, coordinating and editing scholars' contributions and ensuring the academic quality of the series. Duties have been as much administrative as scholarly and have involved collaborating with VCH county committees, and more recently with county trusts and appeals, to raise money and local interest as well as organising the publishing enterprise.

William Page was the first famous and influential General Editor, succeeding H. Arthur Doubleday of the founding publishers, Constable & Co., who had had sole editorial responsibility from 1900 until Page became joint editor in 1902. Page spent 32 years as General Editor until his death in 1934, setting a precedent for longevity in the post which meant that, between 1902 and the retirement of Christopher Currie in 1999, the VCH had only six General Editors: Doubleday, Page, L.F. Salzman, Ralph Pugh, Christopher Elrington and Christopher Currie. The requirement for the General Editor to coordinate the work of increasingly complex county organisations, while acting as an academic figurehead, prompted a change in the role, which was combined with that of Director of the VCH, with Professor Anthony Fletcher and Professor John Beckett each holding the post for five years before the economic climate forced it into abeyance.

The series greatly benefited from the scholarship of a multitude of notable contributors. The consultants brought in by Doubleday to oversee the chapters in general volumes included the Romanist Professor Francis Haverfield, and J.H. Round, whose knowledge of Domesday Book was very well employed in the series. Page's reorganisation of the VCH office in 1904 meant that many of the general chapters were subsequently written by younger scholars, including Frank Stenton who was to become one of the finest medieval historians of the 20th century.

When the VCH was revived in 1933, work began on a new basis with parish histories produced by county teams and far fewer general volumes which contained, nevertheless, much material by established scholars. W.G. Hoskins signed up Rodney Hilton, Joan Thirsk, J.H. Plumb and Jack Simmons to write chapters in the general Leicestershire volumes and, although he wrote little on the county himself, he contributed to Wiltshire volumes, as did Lawrence Stone, Eric Kerridge, F.M.L. Thompson, E.M. Carus-Wilson, Julia de Lacey Mann, Maurice Beresford, Joel Hurstfield and S.T. Bindoff, and two eminent archaeologists, Stuart Piggott and Barrie Cunliffe. Contributors to Cambridgeshire included H.C. Darby, Helen M. Cam, Herbert Butterfield and Edward Miller. Asa Briggs was amongst the Warwickshire authors, while A.G. Dickens and the distinguished regionalist, G.C.F. Forster, contributed to the volume on York.

In the post-war years many young scholars joined the VCH before moving on to other posts. Some, such as Douglas Crowley, Alan Crossley and Robert Dunning, stayed, often rising to county editorships, sometimes writing for more than one county and helping to create the style of topographical writing which has come to characterise the modern VCH. Several, such as Janet Cooper, Nigel Tringham and Patricia Croot, are still involved in VCH work.

William Page (1861–1934)

William Page1 (DLitt), General Editor of the VCH from 1904 until his death, came to the VCH as joint editor in 1902. The longest-serving and most productive General Editor, during his 30-year tenure, Page saw through publication 88 volumes across 35 counties including ten complete county sets. Born in London, he first worked in civil engineering and moved to Australia in 1881, returning to England in 1885 as partner at Hardy & Page record agents, with his brother-in-law William John Hardy. Elected fellow of the Society of Antiquaries in 1887, Page began researching Hertfordshire following a move to St Albans in 1896. His numerous articles brought him to the attention of the VCH which became his life's work, although he also served on the Royal Commission on Historical Monuments (England) and the Historical Manuscripts Commission. In 1932 Page negotiated the transfer of the VCH to the IHR, which ensured the organisation's survival. William Page died on 3 February 1934, his final edited volume, VCH Rutland II being published posthumously in 1935.

L.F. Salzman (1878–1971)

Louis Francis Salzman[2] (CBE, DLitt) was appointed General Editor of the VCH in 1935, following the death of William Page. After the initial enthusiasm for the project and despite Page's best efforts during the interwar years, interest had waned and the IHR had little money to support the project. Nevertheless, Salzman was able to resume work in Oxfordshire and Warwickshire and begin work in Cambridgeshire whilst making solid progress in Sussex, the county with which he had the greatest affinity. When he retired in 1949, Salzman had produced 15 volumes and had exercised a cautious and conservative approach which had preserved the VCH during turbulent times. Away from the VCH, Salzman was particularly productive in Sussex. He joined the council of its archaeological society in 1903, edited 45 volumes of its transactions by 1959 and was one of the co-founders of the Sussex Record Society. Salzman's 1952 work, *Building in England Down to 1540*, influenced his co-founding of the Vernacular Architecture Group, whose meetings he regularly attended until his death in Lewes, Sussex in 1971.

1   *Oxford Dictionary of National Biography (DNB)*, 42 (2004), 335–336.
2   *DNB*, 48 (2004), 790–791.

Ralph Bernard Pugh (1910–1982)

Ralph Bernard Pugh[1] (DLitt) became General Editor of the VCH in 1949, holding the post for 28 years and producing 60 volumes, including completion of the Warwickshire set. It was under Pugh that the VCH began to move away from the model established by Page. Pugh sought to modernise and expand the content of the volumes without altering the established structure. The direct result was that far fewer parishes were covered in each topographical volume and far more volumes were required to complete a county set. Pugh also set up renewable five-year funding agreements with local authorities which stabilised the VCH's finances and, by 1977, funded research in 11 counties. Pugh's career began in 1934 when he was appointed assistant keeper (second class) at the Public Record Office, and in 1937 he founded the records branch of the Wiltshire Archaeological and Natural History Society. Seconded to the Dominions Office during the war, Pugh returned to the PRO in 1946 and established the VCH Wiltshire project, of which he became honorary editor in 1949. After retirement and until his death in London (in December 1982), Pugh continued to research the capital's penal history.

Christopher Elrington (1930–2009)

Christopher Elrington[2] was appointed General Editor in 1977, having joined the VCH in 1954 as part of the central staff under Pugh, and worked for the VCH in some capacity for the entirety of his career. During his 17 years as General Editor, the VCH produced some 42 volumes on 12 counties and continued the trend established by Pugh of significantly expanded parish treatments, especially of settlement and landscape history. From 1961, Elrington served as Gloucestershire County Editor producing two volumes of the Gloucester series before he and his family reluctantly relocated to London to allow him to take up the position of Deputy Editor. A highly adept and respected editor, Elrington was also extremely successful in bringing the VCH to a new audience through low-cost reprints and in managing and maintaining the often fragile network of regional funding arrangements in a climate of constrained local authority spending. Having, upon retirement, established the County History Trust to support the VCH, in 1996 he embarked on the fundraising 'Hike for History', a walk of 1260 miles which took in every English county. He continued to work, producing two volumes of Feet of Fines, and editing and compiling indexes for record publications until his death on 3 August 2009.

1   *DNB*, 45 (2004), 514–515.
2   *Guardian*, 15 Sept. 2009 (obit.).

Christopher Currie (born 1948)

Christopher Currie became General Editor in 1994, having been Assistant Editor in Staffordshire from 1972 and having joined the central office as Deputy Editor in 1978. During his six years as General Editor, under steadily increasing financial difficulties, the VCH produced nine volumes, completed research on Cambridgeshire and revived work on Northamptonshire and Durham. Currie, who as Deputy Editor had been largely responsible for introducing new technology for research, writing and production, as General Editor fostered plans for a digitised version of the VCH and a pilot project for the funding of the VCH by the HLF, both schemes that came to fruition later. He also encouraged new county partnerships with local universities and funding trusts. After his retirement, he worked until 2002 as Consultant Editor, editing chapters for volumes on nine counties and contributing to Middlesex XII on Chelsea. Currie was president of the Vernacular Architecture Group from 2007 to 2011 and continues to serve the VCH as a trustee of the County History Trust.

Francis John Haverfield (1860–1919)

Francis John Haverfield[1] was among the first of the professional scholars commissioned by Doubleday to write chapters for the newly established VCH. From 1884, as sixth-form master at Lancing College, Haverfield had pursued research into a wide range of subjects, before settling on the archaeology and epigraphy of Roman Britain and becoming an authority on them. In 1892, and with a growing reputation, Haverfield returned to Oxford, where he had obtained his degree and took up a position as a senior student and tutor at Christ Church. During that period Doubleday asked him to contribute the chapters on Romano-British remains for all VCH general volumes; he was involved from the outset, providing an entry for the very first VCH volume, *Hampshire* I, and in all volumes containing a chapter on Romano-British remains, appearing as its author. Most of Haverfield's VCH entries were included in volumes published before 1907 when he became Camden Professor of Ancient History at Oxford. His entry for Shropshire appeared in *VCH Shropshire* I (1908) and he used his work for a planned single volume for six northern counties elsewhere.

---

1   *DNB*, 25 (2004), 856–857.

John Horace Round (1854–1928)

John Horace Round[1] was another expert scholar identified by Doubleday as being able to produce chapters for VCH general volumes. Round had obtained his degree from Balliol College, Oxford in 1878. He developed a great interest in the documents relating to English medieval government and in the importance of compiling accurate family histories to the understanding of particular localities. His early work followed these themes, with articles on Colchester's entry in the Domesday Book in 1882 and papers in the two volumes published in 1888 to mark Domesday's 800th anniversary. It was after he moved to London in 1887 that Round's Domesday expertise was harnessed as an essential component of the VCH project. Between 1900 and 1908 he produced 12 county introductions to the Domesday texts, which were printed in translation in the VCH volumes, and he edited many texts by other contributors. Not only has Round's work on Domesday remained central to VCH research methods, but so has his influence on charting the histories of families and their landholdings, with 'manorial descents' remaining one of the best-known features of VCH parish histories.

Image courtesy of Royal Historical Society

Sir Frank Merry Stenton (1880–1967)

Sir Frank Merry Stenton[2] was entrusted to write the sections on Domesday Book for the counties which J.H. Round was unable to undertake due to illness. Stenton gained a first class honours degree in history from Keble College, Oxford in 1902, and began working for the VCH on the Domesday entries for the counties of the East Midlands; Derbyshire, Nottinghamshire, Northamptonshire and Rutland. Working for the VCH enhanced Stenton's reputation and, in 1912, after joining Reading University College as a local history research fellow, he was appointed to the chair of modern history which he retained until his elevation to vice-chancellor in 1946. He continued his association with the VCH, producing Domesday sections for three further counties between 1924 and 1939 in addition to the books for which he is best known, including *The First Century of English Feudalism, 1066–1166* (1932) and *Anglo-Saxon England* (1943). Regarded as one of the finest medieval historians of the 20th century, Stenton also wrote for the Lincoln and Northamptonshire record societies and contributed to the first volume produced by the English Place Name Society in 1924.

1   *DNB*, 47 (2004), 943–946.
2   *DNB*, 52 (2004), 405–407.

Image courtesy of Centre for English Local History, University of Leicester

William George Hoskins (1908–1992)

William George Hoskins[1] (CBE, DLitt) played a central role in the revival of the VCH Leicestershire series which had stalled after the publication of volume I in 1907, although he was unsuccessful in restarting work in Devon. Returning in 1946 to University College, Leicester, where he had lectured in economics between 1931 and 1941, Hoskins — together with Jack Simmons and F.L. Attenborough — established the first university department of English Local History. With the research freedom the department allowed, and supported by Simmons and Attenborough, Hoskins set about organising the Leicestershire VCH. As honorary County Editor he recruited a local committee, compiled a list of contributors for the series and helped raise the requisite funding. He also edited volumes II and III of the revived series before leaving Leicester for Oxford in 1952. At Oxford Hoskins produced the works for which he is best known and which have proved such an inspiration for all those concerned with understanding English localities: *The Making of the English Landscape* (1955); *The Midland Peasant* (1957); and the 1953 article 'The rebuilding of rural England, 1570–1640'.

Image courtesy of English Heritage

Sir Barry Cunliffe (born 1939)

Sir Barry Cunliffe, Professor of European Archaeology, University of Oxford 1972–2007, became involved in archaeology, excavating with local groups on the chalk downs of Hampshire and Sussex before going to Cambridge University. While an assistant lecturer at Bristol University (1963–6) and Director of Excavations at Bath, he realised the superb quality of Francis Haverfield's VCH contribution, especially on Roman Bath in *VCH Somerset* I, the basis for all future research on the Roman spa town. When Professor of Archaeology at the University of Southampton (1966–72), Sir Barry was asked by Elizabeth Crittall to help produce a narrative for *VCH Wiltshire* I. A gazetteer, mainly by Leslie Grinsell, had been published as volume I, part 1 in 1957, but part 2, by Barry Cunliffe, Stuart Piggott and Desmond Bonney, did not follow until 1973. Such long delays demonstrated the difficulty of producing an archaeology volume, partly because of the escalating rate of discovery, so this volume was the only one of its kind ever published. Sir Barry returned to the Hampshire chalk land to develop a programme on Roman settlement (1997–2006). This used Francis Haverfield's first VCH essay (on Roman Hampshire in *VCH Hampshire* I) as its primary source — a vivid reminder of the quality of Haverfield's scholarship.

---

1   *DNB*, 28 (2004), 242-244; J Beckett 'W.G. Hoskins and the Victoria County History in Leicestershire', *Trans. Leicestershire Archaeol. And Hist. Soc.*, 85 (2011)

CONTRIBUTORS 2007–12

A supplement to the lists in *Supplement to the General Introduction* (1990) and *The Little Big Red Book* (2008).

Virginia Bainbridge, WILTSHIRE XVIII, OXFORDSHIRE XVII
John Beckett, NORTHAMPTON VI
James Bettley, ESSEX XI
Peter Boyden, ESSEX XI
Cynthia Brown, NORTHAMPTON VI
Antonia Catchpole, OXFORD XVI
John Chandler, WILTSHIRE XVIII
Nicholas Cooper, OXFORD XVI
Carol Davidson Cragoe, SUSSEX V.2
Patricia E.C. Croot, MIDDLESEX XIII
D.A. Crowley, WILTSHIRE XVIII
S.A. Draper, GLOUCESTER XII
Shirley Durgan, ESSEX XI
C.R. Elrington, SUSSEX V.2
Herbert Eiden, ESSEX XI
M.W. Greenslade, STAFFORD X
N.M. Herbert, GLOUCESTER XII
A.R.J. Juřica, GLOUCESTER XII
G.H.R. Kent, EAST RIDING IX

James Lee, WILTSHIRE XVIII
C.P. Lewis, SUSSEX V.2
R.A. Meeson, STAFFORD X
S.A. Mileson, OXFORD XVI
Peter Mounfield, NORTHAMPTON VI
David Neave, EAST RIDING VIII, IX
Susan Neave, EAST RIDING VIII, IX
Nicholas Orme, CORNWALL II
Oliver Padel, CORNWALL II
Mark Page, OXFORD XVI, XVII
R.B. Peberdy, OXFORD XVI
Paul Rusiecki, ESSEX XI
Andrew Senter, ESSEX XI
M.C. Siraut, SOMERSET X
Carrie Smith, WILTSHIRE XVIII
Simon Townley, OXFORD XVI, XVII
C.C. Thornton, ESSEX XI
Dorothy Treasure, WILTSHIRE XVIII
N.J. Tringham, STAFFORD X
A.P.M. Wright, SUSSEX V.2

Central VCH Editorial team in 2012

Miles Taylor (Director, IHR), Elizabeth Williamson (Executive Editor), A.T. Thacker (Consultant Editor), Matthew Bristow (Research Manager), Jessica Davies (Publications Manager), Rebecca Read (Administrator).

www.victoriacountyhistory.ac.uk

VOLUMES PUBLISHED SINCE 2000

2000: ESSEX,
BIBLIOGRAPHY
SECOND SUPPLEMENT

2001: ESSEX,
VOLUME X

2001: GLOUCESTER,
VOLUME IX

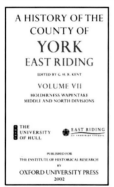

2002: YORK EAST RIDING,
VOLUME VII

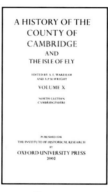

2002: CAMBRIDGE & ELY,
VOLUME X

2002: WILTSHIRE,
VOLUME XVII

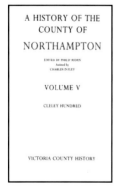

2002: NORTHAMPTON,
VOLUME V

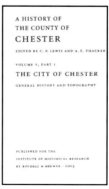

2003: CITY OF CHESTER,
VOLUME V, PART 1

2003: STAFFORD,
VOLUME IX

VOLUMES PUBLISHED SINCE 2000

A HISTORY OF
THE COUNTY OF
SOMERSET
EDITED BY R. W. DUNNING

VOLUME VIII
**THE POLDENS
AND THE LEVELS**

PUBLISHED FOR THE
INSTITUTE OF HISTORICAL RESEARCH

2004: SOMERSET,
VOLUME VIII

A HISTORY OF
THE COUNTY OF
MIDDLESEX
EDITED BY PATRICIA E.C. CROOT

VOLUME XII
CHELSEA

PUBLISHED FOR THE
INSTITUTE OF HISTORICAL RESEARCH
BY BOYDELL & BREWER · 2004

2004: MIDDLESEX,
VOLUME XII

A HISTORY OF
THE COUNTY OF
OXFORD
EDITED BY SIMON TOWNLEY

VOLUME XIV
**WITNEY AND ITS
TOWNSHIPS**
BAMPTON HUNDRED PART TWO

PUBLISHED FOR THE
INSTITUTE OF HISTORICAL RESEARCH
BY BOYDELL & BREWER · 2004

2004: OXFORD,
VOLUME XIV

A HISTORY OF
THE COUNTY OF
DURHAM
EDITED BY GILLIAN COOKSON

VOLUME IV
DARLINGTON

PUBLISHED FOR THE
INSTITUTE OF HISTORICAL RESEARCH
BY BOYDELL & BREWER · 2005

2005: DURHAM,
VOLUME IV

A HISTORY OF
THE COUNTY OF
CHESTER
EDITED BY C. P. LEWIS AND A. T. THACKER

VOLUME V, PART 2
THE CITY OF CHESTER
CULTURE, BUILDINGS, INSTITUTIONS

PUBLISHED FOR THE
INSTITUTE OF HISTORICAL RESEARCH
BY BOYDELL & BREWER · 2005

2005: CHESTER,
VOLUME V, PART 2

A HISTORY OF
THE COUNTY OF
OXFORD
EDITED BY SIMON TOWNLEY

VOLUME XV
**CARTERTON, MINSTER
LOVELL, AND ENVIRONS**
BAMPTON HUNDRED PART THREE

PUBLISHED FOR THE
INSTITUTE OF HISTORICAL RESEARCH
BY BOYDELL & BREWER · 2006

2006: OXFORD,
VOLUME XV

THE COUNTY OF
SOMERSET
EDITED BY R. W. DUNNING

VOLUME IX
**GLASTONBURY AND
STREET**

PUBLISHED FOR THE
INSTITUTE OF HISTORICAL RESEARCH
BY BOYDELL & BREWER · 2006

2006: SOMERSET,
VOLUME IX

A HISTORY OF
THE COUNTY OF
NORTHAMPTON

VOLUME VI
MODERN INDUSTRY

PUBLISHED FOR THE
INSTITUTE OF HISTORICAL RESEARCH
BY BOYDELL & BREWER · 2007

2007: NORTHAMPTON,
VOLUME VI

A HISTORY OF
THE COUNTY OF
STAFFORD
EDITED BY NIGEL J. TRINGHAM

VOLUME X
**TUTBURY AND
NEEDWOOD FOREST**

PUBLISHED FOR THE
INSTITUTE OF HISTORICAL RESEARCH
BY BOYDELL & BREWER · 2007

2007: STAFFORD,
VOLUME X

VOLUMES PUBLISHED SINCE 2000

A HISTORY OF
THE COUNTY OF
YORK: EAST RIDING

VOLUME VIII

EAST BUCKROSE:
SLEDMERE AND THE
NORTHERN WOLDS

DAVID NEAVE AND SUSAN NEAVE

PUBLISHED FOR THE
INSTITUTE OF HISTORICAL RESEARCH
BY BOYDELL & BREWER · 2008

**2008: YORK: EAST RIDING,
VOLUME VIII**

A HISTORY OF
THE COUNTY OF
SUSSEX

EDITED BY C. P. LEWIS

VOLUME V PART 2

LITTLEHAMPTON AND
DISTRICT

(ARUNDEL RAPE, SOUTH-EASTERN PART,
COMPRISING POLING HUNDRED)

PUBLISHED FOR THE
INSTITUTE OF HISTORICAL RESEARCH
BY BOYDELL & BREWER · 2009

**2009: SUSSEX,
VOLUME V, PART 2**

A HISTORY OF
THE COUNTY OF
MIDDLESEX

EDITED BY PATRICIA E.C. CROOT with
ALAN THACKER AND ELIZABETH WILLIAMSON

VOLUME XIII

CITY OF WESTMINSTER
PART 1

PUBLISHED FOR THE
INSTITUTE OF HISTORICAL RESEARCH
BY BOYDELL & BREWER · 2009

**2009: WESTMINSTER,
VOLUME XIII, PART 1**

A HISTORY OF
THE COUNTY OF
GLOUCESTER

VOLUME XII

NEWENT AND MAY HILL

A. R. J. JURICA

PUBLISHED FOR THE
INSTITUTE OF HISTORICAL RESEARCH
BY BOYDELL & BREWER · 2010

**2010: GLOUCESTER,
VOLUME XII**

A HISTORY OF
THE COUNTY OF
CORNWALL

VOLUME II

RELIGIOUS HISTORY
TO 1560

BY NICHOLAS ORME
with a contribution from Oliver Padel

PUBLISHED FOR THE
INSTITUTE OF HISTORICAL RESEARCH
BY BOYDELL & BREWER · 2010

**2010: CORNWALL,
VOLUME II**

A HISTORY OF
THE COUNTY OF
SOMERSET

EDITED BY MARY SIRAUT

VOLUME X

CASTLE CARY AND
THE BRUE–CARY WATERSHED

PUBLISHED FOR THE
INSTITUTE OF HISTORICAL RESEARCH
BY BOYDELL & BREWER · 2010

**2010: SOMERSET,
VOLUME X**

A HISTORY OF
THE COUNTY OF
WILTSHIRE

EDITED BY VIRGINIA BAINBRIDGE

VOLUME XVIII

CRICKLADE AND ENVIRONS

PUBLISHED FOR THE
INSTITUTE OF HISTORICAL RESEARCH
BY BOYDELL & BREWER · 2011

**2011: WILTSHIRE,
VOLUME XVII**

A HISTORY OF
THE COUNTY OF
OXFORD

EDITED BY SIMON TOWNLEY

VOLUME XVI

HENLEY-ON-THAMES
AND ENVIRONS

PUBLISHED FOR THE
INSTITUTE OF HISTORICAL RESEARCH
BY BOYDELL & BREWER · 2011

**2011: OXFORD,
VOLUME XVI**

VOLUMES PUBLISHED SINCE 2000

JUBILEE YEAR PUBLICATIONS

A HISTORY OF
THE COUNTY OF
ESSEX

EDITED BY CHRISTOPHER C. THORNTON
ASSISTED BY HERBERT EITON

VOLUME XI

CLACTON, WALTON AND
FRINTON

NORTH-EAST ESSEX SEASIDE RESORTS

PUBLISHED FOR THE
INSTITUTE OF HISTORICAL RESEARCH
BY BOYDELL & BREWER · 2012

A HISTORY OF
THE COUNTY OF
YORK: EAST RIDING

VOLUME VIII

EAST BUCKROSE:
SLEDMERE AND THE
NORTHERN WOLDS

DAVID NEAVE AND SUSAN NEAVE

A HISTORY OF
THE COUNTY OF
OXFORD

EDITED BY SIMON TOWNLEY

VOLUME XVII

BROADWELL, LANGFORD,
AND KELMSCOTT

BAMPTON HUNDRED, PART FOUR

PUBLISHED FOR THE
INSTITUTE OF HISTORICAL RESEARCH
BY BOYDELL & BREWER · 2012

2012: ESSEX,
VOLUME XI

2012: YORKSHIRE
EAST RIDING,
VOLUME IX

2012: OXFORD,
VOLUME XVII

The VCH publications programme

Over forthcoming academic years there will be volumes from Staffordshire (XI), Shropshire (IV), Northamptonshire (VII & VIII), followed by volumes from Wiltshire (XIX), Durham (V), Derbyshire (III and IV), Somerset (XI and XII), Oxfordshire (XVIII), Essex (XII) and Gloucestershire (XIII). There are also some counties in the initial planning and researching stages and it is hoped that a combination of volunteer effort and collaborative working will enable projects in counties such as Hampshire, Cumbria, Leicestershire to become red volumes in time.

The VCH staff c. 2010 standing in front of the old Orange Street office. The building has long since been demolished and a modern office block stands in its prime central London location. From left to right, Jessica Davies, Elizabeth Williamson, Alan Thacker, John Beckett and Matthew Bristow.

THE VCH IN THE 21ST CENTURY

THE VCH SINCE 2000

During the last 12 years many aspects of the VCH have been transformed. In 2000, as the VCH developed its ambitious national England's Past for Everyone project, the first General Editor also to carry the title of Director was appointed. Professor Anthony Fletcher's aim was to make the VCH a transparent organisation attractive to potential funders, and especially to the HLF which had provided a grant towards a pilot project in 1999. A large part of the task was to develop the next phase of the University of London's application to the HLF, by forging and cementing financial and academic partnerships, and by clarifying how the VCH maintained its academic standards.

Many of the changes necessary to gain HLF support were already underway when project development began. The need to apply for such funds had been instigated by the gradual withdrawal of other types of funding from established VCH counties, particularly by local authorities. County trusts and appeals proved increasingly important; amongst the earliest were the pioneering Essex, Northamptonshire and Oxfordshire VCH trusts, founded in the 1990s, followed by the Derbyshire trust of 2001 and then others. Partnerships with universities were developed to support local VCH staff, for example with the universities of Durham, Essex, Gloucestershire, Northampton and the University of the West of England (Wiltshire VCH), or to further EPE projects in Bristol (UWE), Cornwall (Exeter), Durham (Sunderland) and Herefordshire (Gloucestershire).

As far as the outside world was concerned, the most obvious change after 2000 was to VCH publications. A move from Oxford University Press to a new publisher, Boydell & Brewer, in October 2001, was accompanied by a fresh design created for the books in 2002 by Tony Kitzinger. The new design gave expression to a clearer framework of content within coherent, well-signposted sections including social history, Professor Fletcher's own subject. The first book to appear in the new style — which was well received — was *VCH Cheshire* V, part 1 (2003). During the same period, public acquaintance with VCH materials and information was increased by means of a newsletter (from 2001), by free online access to VCH's publications digitised on the IHR's British History Online (from 2004), and two key elements of the HLF pilot project — the first VCH website and the first VCH paperback study (*The Townscape of Darlington*, 2003).

Anthony Fletcher retired in 2003. By autumn 2005, when Professor John Beckett was seconded from the University of Nottingham as second Director and General Editor of the VCH, the HLF had granted the VCH funding but the EPE project had only just begun. Perhaps John Beckett's most daunting task of the many undertaken for that project was making sure that 15 paperback books were researched, written and published from scratch within five years. Not only did Professor Beckett have to see the EPE project through, but he was also charged by the University of London with developing a transformed VCH even further by encouraging new VCH work in as many counties as possible. By the time he returned to Nottingham in 2010, he had established projects on EPE lines in six more counties: East Sussex (Brighton and Hove), Hampshire, Cumbria (Cumberland and Westmorland), Nottinghamshire and Leicestershire. He had also ensured work could continue in counties such as Herefordshire, Kent and Cornwall, brought into the VCH as part of the EPE project, as well as in the long-established counties such as Staffordshire and Wiltshire. His achievement in so short a time was tremendous.

ENGLAND'S PAST FOR EVERYONE

In June 1999, almost exactly a century after the organisation was founded, the VCH made an application to the Heritage Lottery Fund (established in 1993) for funds to start a pilot project which would assess the options available for making its vast body of published material and highly respected research available in new formats. The HLF award, combined with matching funding, amounted to over £400,000 and enabled the VCH to run a pilot development project in County Durham and Oxfordshire. That project examined how information presented in VCH red volumes could be made more accessible to a wider audience, whilst maintaining the standards for which the VCH was known. It also included the VCH's first foray into the provision of educational resources, with primary school teaching materials — focusing on Codford in Wiltshire, Warter in the East Riding of Yorkshire and the city of Bristol — posted on a newly created web resource 'History Footsteps'.

The project, which ran between autumn 2000 and autumn 2001, led, in July 2003, to an application to the HLF for a major award to fund a five-year national project entitled 'England's Past for Everyone'. The bid was successful and, early in 2005, an award was made of £3,374,000, a sum which, when supplemented by the matching funding contributions of many partners, increased the total to nearly £6 million.

The project officially started on 1 September 2005, managed by a newly assembled project team based at the VCH's central office in the IHR. During the life of the project, which finished at the end of April 2010, research was conducted by established and newly formed VCH teams in ten English counties or localities: Cornwall, Exmoor, Bristol, Wiltshire, Sussex, Kent, Oxfordshire, Derbyshire, Herefordshire and County Durham. Their work resulted in 15 new paperback books, the England's Past for Everyone series, on themes ranging from the pre-Reformation story of Cornish Christianity to the complete history of Codford, a small village in West Wiltshire, and the story of the growth of Sunderland from a centre of monastic scholarly endeavour in the 7th century to its rise and decline as a port and industrial city.

The EPE project not only aimed to make the work of the VCH accessible to a new and wider audience, it also sought to include that audience in the research process and in the generation of the histories of the localities involved. To that end the project included a substantial programme of training and volunteer engagement which saw more than 300 volunteers working across the ten projects on a range of activities, including archival research, document transcription and historic building survey. Much of their research material and results, and those compiled by the team leaders, were made available as an interactive web resource and remain available through the VCH Explore website.

The EPE project also built on the work of the 'History Footsteps' pilot project, involving more than 700 primary school pupils throughout the country and creating an online resource of Key Stage 1, 2 and 3 teaching materials. They can be found online on the EPE Schools Learning Zone.

The project was transformative, changing the way in which the VCH works with others and how it presents its research to a wider audience through personal engagement and the internet. The changes initiated by EPE are still continuing to evolve, with VCH activity being reawakened in many more counties since 2000.

VOLUNTEERING AND THE VCH

Contributing to the work of the Victoria County History on a voluntary basis is not new to the organisation. Throughout its long history, the VCH has received contributions for publication from scholars not employed by the organisation and the position of County Editor has often been held on an honorary basis, as it was by Ralph Pugh in Wiltshire in the early 1950s and is by Mary Siraut in Somerset at present. The VCH has also made use of volunteer groups working with a County Editor to reduce the time required to cover the requisite sources needed to construct a parish entry, most notably in Derbyshire where Philip Riden's volunteer groups have been active across the county for much of the last ten years.

It was the England's Past for Everyone project which dramatically increased the level of volunteer engagement with the work of the VCH. Central to the mission of the project was the direct involvement of local communities in the generation of the history of their locality. More than 250 volunteers from across the ten study areas participated in a range of research activities during the project's life. The volunteers received expert training from VCH County Editors, EPE staff and expert consultants. They analysed censuses, transcribed wills, examined historic newspapers, surveyed historic buildings and villages, recorded landscapes, undertook archaeological excavation, recorded oral testimony, took photographs and mounted web content. Their hard work and endeavour was crucial to the project's success, allowing the rapid completion of research and the production of 15 paperback books and other EPE outputs in under five years. We hope they enjoyed learning about local history and the experience of working with other enthusiasts.

The end of EPE did not mean the end of volunteer activity, for it has been integrated into VCH methods of working, with new volunteer groups established in Hampshire, Herefordshire, Cumbria and Leicestershire and the successful Oxfordshire wills group continuing to transcribe probate records. In addition, offers from independent scholars to conduct research voluntarily have recently contributed to VCH work in Shropshire and the East Riding of Yorkshire.

In order to promote further VCH work involving local societies and volunteer groups, the VCH website now includes an online guide to writing VCH parish and urban histories and a Volunteer Toolkit which explains how to set up, market, manage and evaluate a volunteer programme. Additional guidelines for individuals and volunteers are planned for 2003.

Volunteers in Herefordshire undertake building survey work as part of the EPE project. Their work was integral to both the paperback books produced on Ledbury and the associated website.

DIGITAL PROJECTS

Crucial to the HLF's requirements for the EPE project was a strong web presence for the VCH. The VCH website, with the authority of an academic domain name since 2006, now communicates with all those interested in local and family history, heritage and in particular localities, as well as publishing interim results of county research long before hard-copy publication. Also available digitally are numerous local history resources on VCH Explore and the Schools Learning Zone and many VCH red books on British History Online.

The Victoria County History Website

The VCH launched its first website (www.englandpast.net) in 1999, just in advance of its first application to the HLF. That site provided a platform to communicate the VCH's history and current work, and space for 'micro-sites' for each active county to publicise its activities and web-mount draft parish entries for comment before publication. The

VCH website also provided guidance on how to compile the history of a house, school or family and how to 'Get Started' in researching and writing a parish history.

The site was enhanced in 2006 and again in 2011 when it was underpinned by the Drupal content management system. In addition to the sections and structures familiar from the original site, the latest version of the VCH website includes greatly expanded sections on how to write a parish or urban history for the VCH, and how to become the author of an EPE paperback. It also has a searchable database detailing which parishes the VCH has covered and enhanced micro-sites for all of the English counties. From 2013 the site is expected to include a commercial image gallery, which will make the vast collection of photographs taken for VCH volumes available for purchase and licensing.

VCH Explore

As well as a communications site, the HLF encouraged the creation of an Explore site to give direct access to the material collected and created by county teams and volunteers, and used to write paperback volumes. The resources were organised into 'items' (an historic building, site, person or event) and populated with 'assets' (documents, photographs, maps, plans, transcriptions and so on). Every item was geo-located using Google maps and could be browsed geographically or by EPE project.

In 2010, the EPE Explore site was rebuilt and the material dissociated from individual EPE projects, in order to allow contributions from every VCH county nationwide. The material was reorganised thematically, each theme enabling the user to view the items in a wider historical context. The Google maps interface has been retained. During 2012, the Explore site will enter its third iteration, which will see its functionality improved and the domain changed to affiliate it more closely with the whole VCH project. By the end of 2012 it will be found at www.victoriacountyhistory.ac.uk/Explore.

Schools Learning Zone

The EPE project also produced an online collection of resources, tailored to the teaching of local history at primary school level and directly related to the research undertaken for the paperback book series. These primary sources, lesson plans, teacher's packs and interactive resources were suitable for Key Stages 1–3 of the National Curriculum. They built on the work of the EPE pilot project, which saw the creation of the 'History Footsteps' website with schools' resources relating to Warter in the East Riding of Yorkshire, Codford in Wiltshire and Bristol. The EPE schools resources are still available online and can be found at http://englandspastforeveryone.org.uk/schools.

Welcome to Schools Learning Zone

This website offers FREE educational material for teachers and pupils!

Schools Learning Zone has been developed by the Victoria County History's Heritage Lottery-funded project *England's Past for Everyone*.

Teaching Material

Interactive Resources

Teachers can download packs of educational resources, activities, timelines and lesson plans. The material is cross-curricular and makes links to the National Curriculum.

Featured Items

Elizabeth I's Coat of Arms: have a look at this interactive image to find out what the different parts of the coat of arms mean.

Slavery Trail, Bristol: follows a route through the city and includes a number of sites with links to the Transatlantic Slave Trade

Diversity Through Time, Bristol: from medieval Jews to modern day asylum seekers.

A screenshot taken from the Schools Learning Zone *website, now archived, part of the* England's Past for Everyone *project.*

British History Online

Between 2003 and 2004, the VCH red volumes formed one of a group of resources included in the IHR's British History Online (BHO) pilot project. The project, supported by a grant of £235,000 from the Andrew W. Mellon Foundation, aimed to provide a digital library of text and information about people, places and businesses from the medieval and early modern period; it included resources from the IHR's Centre for Metropolitan History and external partners such as the History of Parliament and TNA. During the pilot project 22 VCH volumes were digitised in their entirety and converted to a navigable XML format which allowed users to move between the various subsections of the VCH entries as they would if using the hard copy volume. Such was the success of the BHO pilot project that two further phases of digitisation were undertaken between 2004 and 2008, with each phase supported by additional grants of £495,000 from the Mellon Foundation.At the time of writing, 163 volumes of the VCH have been digitised as part of the BHO project and form part of an extensive digital collection which includes volumes of *The Survey of London*, the complete first edition of the Ordnance Survey and, from 2013, will display the county inventories of the Royal Commission on Historical Monuments of England. The VCH volumes can be used free of charge, independently, or in conjunction with most of the other resources on www.british-history.ac.uk.

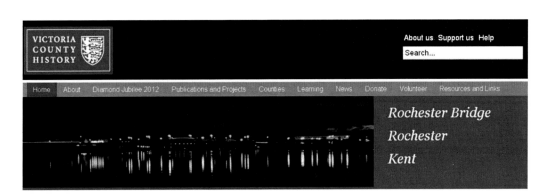

Welcome to the Victoria County History

Founded in 1899 and originally dedicated to Queen Victoria, the VCH is an encyclopaedic record of England's places and people from earliest times to the present day. Based at the Institute of Historical Research in the University of London since 1933, the VCH is written by historians working in counties across England and is without doubt the greatest publishing project in English local history.

Counties

News and events

Leicestershire volunteers study contrasting villages
Leicestershire volunteers braved the rain (having missed the hail and thunder by a few hours) to study two...

Lords and Peasants in the Medieval Countryside - a National Trust Study Day
The theme of the study day is medieval rural society with a particular focus on Sussex. Four experts on the...

Lewes before Lewes
Professor John Blair, The Queen's College, Oxford. Lewes before the foundation of King Alfred's...

Did You Know?

Since the days when spiders were regarded as a cure for fen ague and as weather prophets for the husbandman little attention was paid to them in the county until the latter half of the 19th century.

History of the County of Cambridge and the Isle of Ely. Volume 1 (1938)

Buy this volume

EPE PUBLICATIONS
A new approach to local history publishing

The England's Past for Everyone project produced, as one of its published outputs, a series of 15 paperback books covering a variety of themes and focusing on places and people. The series, characterised by well-illustrated narratives and text boxes, is based on the high standards of documentary research and fieldwork expected from the VCH. The paperbacks were published by Phillimore & Co Ltd.

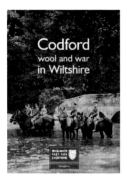

CODFORD: WOOL AND WAR IN WILTSHIRE
JOHN CHANDLER
ISBN 978-1-86077-441-6   PUB. 2007

Codford village and its surroundings are not only beautiful, they are also rich in history. First mentioned in 901, the village's later development was subject to the twin influences of road and river. With chapters discussing farming, landowners, church and community and the impact of two world wars, this fascinating look into Codford's rich past will evoke the history of many similar places.

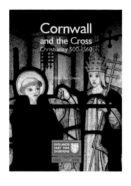

CORNWALL AND THE CROSS: CHRISTIANITY 500–1560
NICHOLAS ORME
ISBN 978-1-86077-468-3   PUB. 2007

Cornwall's place names and churches are unique. They commemorate a great number of local saints such as St Austell, St Ives and St Just. This book explains how the Cornish developed distinctive traditions while fully sharing in the Christianity of western Europe; how Cornwall came to be Christian after the end of the Roman Empire; and how its religious history developed through the Middle Ages and into the Reformation.

BRISTOL: ETHNIC MINORITIES AND THE CITY 1000–2001
MADGE DRESSER, PETER FLEMING
ISBN 978-1-86077-477-5   PUB. 2007

This pioneering study offers new insights into the experiences of foreigners who came to Bristol. It bears witness to their many stories and begins to piece together how these migrants have affected the city's own sense of itself. Full of archival material, and interviews with Bristolians themselves, this is the first time that immigration and ethnic minorities have been explored in such depth over the entire recorded history of a single city.

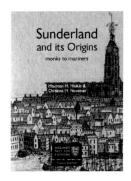

SUNDERLAND AND ITS ORIGINS: MONKS TO MARINERS
MAUREEN M MIEKLE, CHRISTINE M NEWMAN
ISBN 978-1-86077-479-9   PUB. 2007

Sunderland was once the seat of one of the most important centres of learning in the whole of Europe. This book not only tells the story of Bede's scholarly world and the Wearmouth monastery, but for the first time maps the history of the surrounding settlements, as Wearsiders carved a living from the sea, the river and the increasingly important coal trade.

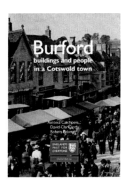

BURFORD: BUILDINGS AND PEOPLE IN A COTSWOLD TOWN
ANTONIA CATCHPOLE, DAVID CLARK, ROBERT PEBERDY
ISBN978-1-86077-488-1   PUB. 2008

This book explores Burford's stunning buildings and the rich history behind them, from its creation by medieval planners and its role in the Cotswold wool trade, to its later history as a small market town. Never before have the buildings been studied in such depth. The inclusion of a gazetteer of the buildings on the main streets makes this an indispensable guide for locals and visitors alike.

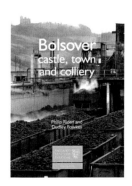

BOLSOVER: CASTLE, TOWN AND COLLIERY
PHILIP RIDEN, DUDLEY FOWKES
ISBN 978-1-86077-485-0   PUB. 2008

Bolsover is famous for its castle and its colliery, the boldest elements in the rich history of a town that was laid out shortly after the Norman Conquest. This book explores the history of town and parish, from the castle and the Cavendish family, to the model housing of New Bolsover. The book also charts the changing fortunes of Bolsover's communities, from rural origins to post-industrial present.

PARHAM: AN ELIZABETHAN HOUSE AND ITS RESTORATION
JAYNE KIRK
ISBN: 978-1-86077-485-0   PUB. 2009

Parham House lies at the foot of the South Downs, an Elizabethan house with weathered stone walls and a gabled silhouette. This book tells the story of the house and of the three families who owned it for more than 400 years. A previous archive of drawings, letters and other papers has revealed much new evidence, while specially commissioned studies and personal recollections have added yet another perspective.

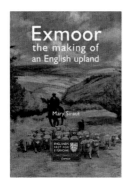

Exmoor: the making of an English upland
Mary Siraut
ISBN: 978-1-86077-597 PUB. 2009

Home to a wide variety of flora and fauna, it is difficult to believe that the scenery we see on Exmoor today is the result of millennia of human intervention . This book looks at the history of both landscape and community in 11 Exmoor parishes, from pre-historic times to present day. The book explores population and migration, the origins of place names and deserted farmsteads, and also includes many new images and reconstruction drawings.

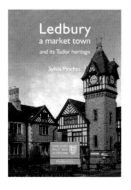

Ledbury: a market town and its tudor heritage
Sylvia Pinches
ISBN: 978-1-86077-598-7 PUB. 2009

This book tells the story of Ledbury from 1558, when Elizabeth 1 confiscated the bishop's manor and estate, through a period of great prosperity in the 16th century, to the present day. It traces the ups and downs of the market town and its resulting physical transformation, including the wide marketplace and streets lined with timber-framed buildings, which still attract visitors today.

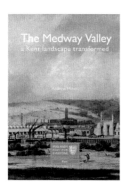

The Medway Valley: a kent landscape transformed
Andrew Hann
ISBN: 978-1-86077-600-7 PUB. 2009

In 1750 the lower Medway Valley was firmly part of Kent's 'Garden of England'. A century later, this agrarian landscape had been transformed into a hive of industry and commerce, yet by the end of the Second World War much of this industry was gone. This book details the changing patterns of work and society and the pivotal role of the river during two centuries of change and upheaval.

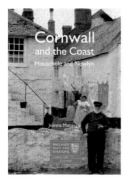

Cornwall and the coast: mousehole and newlyn
Joanna Mattingly
ISBN: 978-1-86077-489-8 PUB. 2009

A favourite Cornish toast at the end of the 18th century was 'fish, tin and copper' and it was the first of these that brought prosperity to the ports of Mousehole and Newlyn. From the medieval watermills of Mousehole, to controversial slum clearance in 20th-century Newlyn, the story of the two villages is told against a backdrop of national concerns, including the English Civil War and the arrival of the railways.

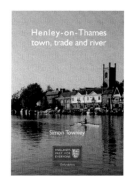

HENLEY-ON-THAMES: TOWN, TRADE AND RIVER
SIMON TOWNLEY
ISBN: 978-1-86077-554-3   PUB. 2009

Henley-on-Thames is best known for its attractive buildings, its 18th-century bridge and its annual Regatta. This book explores Henley and its relationship with the river, from its origins as an inland port, through to its 18th-century development as a coaching centre and its present-day role as a small service, tourist and commuting town. The book casts new light on Henley, allowing visitors and residents alike to view it with fresh eyes.

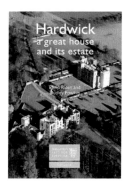

HARDWICK: A GREAT HOUSE AND ITS ESTATE
PHILIP RIDEN, DUDLEY FOWKES
ISBN: 978-1-86077-544-4   PUB. 2009

One of the most magnificent great houses of the Elizabethan period, Hardwick New Hall stands prominently on high ground overlooking the valley of the river Doe Lea in north-east Derbyshire. This book looks at the history of both the halls and the wider estate, the changing fortunes of the Cavendish family and the growth and decline of the coal-mining industry in the area.

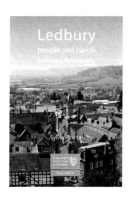

LEDBURY: PEOPLE AND PARISH BEFORE THE REFORMATION
SYLVIA PINCHES
ISBN: 978-1-86077-614-4   PUB. 2010

This book explores the history of Ledbury from earliest times until the middle of the 16th century. Using the evidence of the landscape itself; physical remains; artefacts and buildings; and tantalising glimpses from old documents, it has been possible to chart the history of this market town for nearly 500 years. The story ends in 1558, where our second Ledbury volume takes up the story.

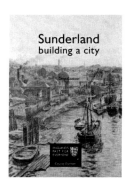

SUNDERLAND: BUILDING A CITY
GILLIAN COOKSON
ISBN: 978-1-86077-547-5   PUB. 2010

This book traces the physical development of Sunderland from medieval settlement to the city of a new millennium. Illustrated with modern and historic photographs and drawings, and specially commissioned maps and plans, it explores Sunderland's spectacular growth as a centre of the coal trade, as a commercial power and port and as a town drawing in many thousands of migrants.

THE FUTURE...

In 2012 there are 22 counties involved in VCH, ten more than in 2000, and 16 have involved volunteers in their work. There is nowhere better than the VCH website to find out about the VCH national network and the steady stream of new publications, researched and written in the counties and edited and prepared for publication in Central Office. The website also offers a vivid picture of activity in each county and an opportunity to read parish and urban histories in progress from all over the country.

The value of the Victoria County History as an enduring enterprise of magnificent scope and great utility has been endorsed by the rededication to H.M. Queen Elizabeth II, by her gracious permission, in this Diamond Jubilee year. We are going forward with a full publishing programme and ideas for making old and new VCH histories available, as well as active fundraising locally and centrally. Our need for funds continues and we hope that all those who value the VCH and love their localities will support our work.

The Victoria County History has always relied on the generous financial support provided by interested charities, individuals and institutions, especially those with strong links in their local areas. Without such support, the VCH would be unable to continue its production of high-quality local history resources in print and online, the result of unrivalled research and the superb work of local history volunteers.

You can request that your gift or legacy contributes to a specific task or programme (such as research or training), or to work in an individual county, town or, where possible, parish. If you are interested in a particular aspect, the Executive Editor, Elizabeth Williamson, would be pleased to discuss how your gift could help develop it (elizabeth.williamson@sas.ac.uk; 020 7862 8777).

A donation can be made through our national or county trusts. Regular support is especially beneficial so please consider giving by regular standing order or direct debit. If you are a UK taxpayer and complete a Gift Aid declaration, the VCH will be able to claim an extra 28p for every pound you donate.

The County History Trust (reg. char. 1043526) is the VCH's central trust. It was founded by the late Christopher Elrington, General Editor (1977–94). It holds money for work in counties which do not yet have their own trust or appeal and helps all counties with small grants.

- Treasurer Dr Paul Seaward, The History of Parliament, 18 Bloomsbury Square, London WC1A 2NS; pseaward@histparl.ac.uk.

County Trusts and Appeals

Local VCH trusts and appeal committees welcome donations to support research, volunteer activity and publications.

The Victoria County History of Cornwall Trust Ltd (reg. char. 05356554)
- Administrator Elaine Henderson, 18 Berrycombe Road, Bodmin, Cornwall PL31 2NS

Cumbria County History Trust (reg. char. 1137379)
- Secretary R.A.A. Brockington, Highland Hall, Renwick, Penrith, CA10 1JL (01768 870352); richard.brockington@mypostoffice.co.uk

Derbyshire VCH Trust (reg. char. 1098339).
- County Editor Philip Riden, School of History, University of Nottingham, University Park, Nottingham, NG7 2RD; philip.riden@nottingham.ac.uk

Durham VCH Trust (reg. char. 1026167).
- c/o VCH, Palace Green Library, Palace Green, Durham, DH1 3RN

Victoria County History of Essex (Appeal) Fund (reg. char. 1038801)
- Hon.Treasurer Martin Stuchfield, Lowe Hill House, Stratford St. Mary, Suffolk CO7 6JX; martinstuchfield@btinternet.com

Gloucestershire County History Trust (reg. char. 1138520)
- Hon. Treasurer Dr James Hodsdon, 49 Pittville Crescent Lane, Cheltenham GL52 2RA

Hampshire Archives Trust VCH Project (reg. char. 294312)
- c/o Hampshire Record Office, Sussex Street, Winchester, SO23 8TH

Herefordshire VCH Trust (reg.char. 1070427)
- c/o Museum Resource and Learning Centre, 58 Friar St, Hereford, HR4 0AS.

Leicestershire VCH Trust (reg.char. 1128575)
- The Secretary, Marc Fitch Historical Institute, 5 Salisbury Road, Leicester, LE1 7QR; jad17@le.ac.uk

Northamptonshire VCH Trust (reg. char. 1051380)
- Hon. Secretary David Harries, c/o County Record Office, Wootton Hall Park, Northampton, NN4 8BQ; David.harries2@btinternet.com or enquiries@northamptonshirerecordsociety.org.uk

The VCH Oxfordshire Trust (reg.char. 1064776)
- Treasurer Liam Tiller, East House, Rokemarsh, Wallingford, Oxon. OX10 6JB; LiamTiller@waitrose.com

Wiltshire VCH Appeal Trust (reg.char. 1102882)
- c/o Wiltshire & Swindon History Centre,Cocklebury Road, Chippenham, Wiltshire SN15 3QN (01249 705516); virginia.bainbridge@uwe.co.uk

Would you consider remembering the VCH in your will? If you are interested in contributing in that way, please contact Heather Dwyer, IHR Development Director, at: development@sas.ac.uk; 020 7862 8791 or read more on the IHR website.